ISO 31000
Complete Self-Assessment Gu

The guidance in this Self-Assessment is based on ISO 31000 best practices and standards in business process architecture, design and quality management. The guidance is also based on the professional judgment of the individual collaborators listed in the Acknowledgments.

http://theartofservice.com
service@theartofservice.com

Table of Contents

About The Art of Service

The Art of Service, Business Process Architects since 2000, is dedicated to helping stakeholders achieve excellence.

Defining, designing, creating, and implementing a process to solve a stakeholders challenge or meet an objective is the most valuable role... In EVERY group, company, organization and department.

Unless you're talking a one-time, single-use project, there should be a process. Whether that process is managed and implemented by humans, AI, or a combination of the two, it needs to be designed by someone with a complex enough perspective to ask the right questions.

Someone capable of asking the right questions and step back and say, 'What are we really trying to accomplish here? And is there a different way to look at it?'

With The Art of Service's Standard Requirements Self-Assessments, we empower people who can do just that — whether their title is marketer, entrepreneur, manager, salesperson, consultant, Business Process Manager, executive assistant, IT Manager, CIO etc... —they are the people who rule the future. They are people who watch the process as it happens, and ask the right questions to make the process work better.

Contact us when you need any support with this Self-Assessment and any help with templates, blue-prints and examples of standard documents you might need:

http://theartofservice.com
service@theartofservice.com

Included Resources - how to access

Included with your purchase of the book is the ISO 31000

Self-Assessment Spreadsheet Dashboard which contains all questions and Self-Assessment areas and auto-generates insights, graphs, and project RACI planning - all with examples to get you started right away.

How? Simply send an email to
access@theartofservice.com
with this books' title in the subject to get the ISO 31000 Self Assessment Tool right away.

You will receive the following contents with New and Updated specific criteria:

- The latest quick edition of the book in PDF
- The latest complete edition of the book in PDF, which criteria correspond to the criteria in...
- The Self-Assessment Excel Dashboard, and...
- Example pre-filled Self-Assessment Excel Dashboard to get familiar with results generation
- In-depth specific Checklists covering the topic
- Project management checklists and templates to assist with implementation

INCLUDES LIFETIME SELF ASSESSMENT UPDATES

Every self assessment comes with Lifetime Updates and Lifetime Free Updated Books. Lifetime Updates is an industry-first feature which allows you to receive verified self assessment updates, ensuring you always have the most accurate information at your fingertips.

Get it now- you will be glad you did - do it now, before you forget.

Send an email to **access@theartofservice.com** with this books' title in the subject to get the ISO 31000 Self Assessment Tool right away.

Purpose of this Self-Assessment

This Self-Assessment has been developed to improve understanding of the requirements and elements of ISO 31000, based on best practices and standards in business process architecture, design and quality management.

It is designed to allow for a rapid Self-Assessment to determine how closely existing management practices and procedures correspond to the elements of the Self-Assessment.

The criteria of requirements and elements of ISO 31000 have been rephrased in the format of a Self-Assessment questionnaire, with a seven-criterion scoring system, as explained in this document.

In this format, even with limited background knowledge of ISO 31000, a manager can quickly review existing operations to determine how they measure up to the standards. This in turn can serve as the starting point of a 'gap analysis' to identify management tools or system elements that might usefully be implemented in the organization to help improve overall performance.

How to use the Self-Assessment

On the following pages are a series of questions to identify to what extent your ISO 31000 initiative is complete in comparison to the requirements set in standards.

To facilitate answering the questions, there is a space in front of each question to enter a score on a scale of '1' to '5'.

1 Strongly Disagree

2 Disagree

3 Neutral

4 Agree

5 Strongly Agree

Read the question and rate it with the following in front of mind:

'In my belief,
the answer to this question is clearly defined'.

There are two ways in which you can choose to interpret this statement;

1. how aware are you that the answer to the question is clearly defined
2. for more in-depth analysis you can choose to gather evidence and confirm the answer to the question. This obviously will take more time, most Self-Assessment users opt for the first way to interpret the question and dig deeper later on based on the outcome of the overall Self-Assessment.

A score of '1' would mean that the answer is not clear at all, where a '5' would mean the answer is crystal clear and defined. Leave emtpy when the question is not applicable or you don't want to answer it, you can skip it without affecting your score. Write your score in the space provided.

After you have responded to all the appropriate statements in each section, compute your average score for that section, using the formula provided, and round to the nearest tenth. Then transfer to the corresponding spoke in the ISO 31000 Scorecard on the second next page of the Self-Assessment.

Your completed ISO 31000 Scorecard will give you a clear presentation of which ISO 31000 areas need attention.

ISO 31000
Scorecard Example

Example of how the finalized Scorecard can look like:

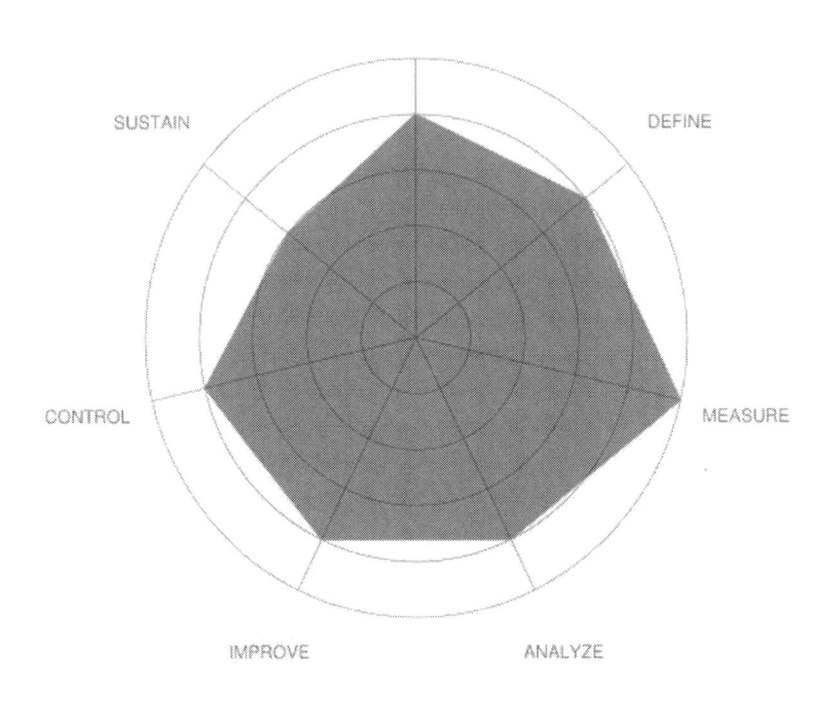

ISO 31000 Scorecard

Your Scores:

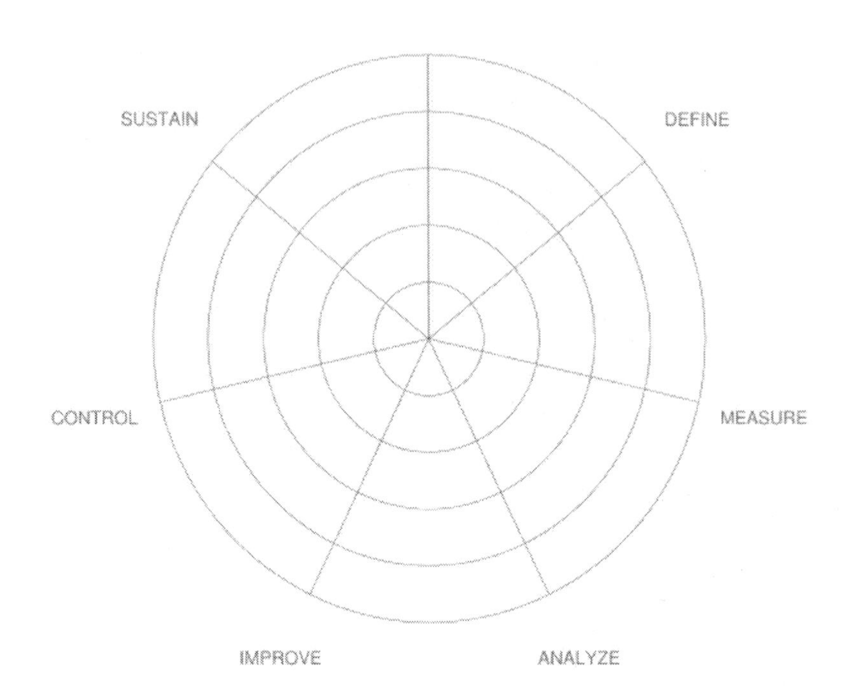

BEGINNING OF THE SELF-ASSESSMENT:

CRITERION #1: RECOGNIZE

INTENT: Be aware of the need for change. Recognize that there is an unfavorable variation, problem or symptom.

In my belief, the answer to this question is clearly defined:

5 Strongly Agree

4 Agree

3 Neutral

2 Disagree

1 Strongly Disagree

1. What level of granularity of information is needed?
<--- Score

2. What situation(s) led to this ISO 31000 Self Assessment?
<--- Score

3. Who else hopes to benefit from it?

<--- Score

4. Is there a minimum set of languages that need to be covered by translation services?
<--- Score

5. Which of the positions on your chart would have a need for accounting information?
<--- Score

6. Can ISO 31000 be modified to meet the needs of large and multi-national organizations?
<--- Score

7. How are the ISO 31000's objectives aligned to the group's overall stakeholder strategy?
<--- Score

8. Are there any specific expectations or concerns about the ISO 31000 team, ISO 31000 itself?
<--- Score

9. How does the enterprise get IT under control corresponding that it delivers the information the enterprise needs?
<--- Score

10. What are the skill sets and staffing needs of an internal audit activity?
<--- Score

11. What tools will your organization need to implement the ERM program?
<--- Score

12. What is de-identified?

<--- Score

13. Does your organization collect personally identifiable information electronically?
<--- Score

14. What keying material needs to be saved for a given application?
<--- Score

15. Is there any corrective action needed?
<--- Score

16. Do you need to form a functional ERM unit?
<--- Score

17. What activities will be part of the event?
<--- Score

18. As a sponsor, customer or management, how important is it to meet goals, objectives?
<--- Score

19. How are you going to measure success?
<--- Score

20. What are the different consequences of different types of fraud events?
<--- Score

21. Has your organization identified its high value assets?
<--- Score

22. Have you articulated reporting elements for the kinds of information you disclose in the event

of an attack?
<--- Score

23. What are the stakeholder objectives to be achieved with ISO 31000?
<--- Score

24. Do you have password policies for enterprise issued mobile devices and/or BYOD mobile devices?
<--- Score

25. What are the expected benefits of ISO 31000 to the stakeholder?
<--- Score

26. Is the program meeting current needs?
<--- Score

27. How much are sponsors, customers, partners, stakeholders involved in ISO 31000? In other words, what are the risks, if ISO 31000 does not deliver successfully?
<--- Score

28. Are needed to adequately protect the information systems that support the operations and assets of your organization?
<--- Score

29. What problems are you facing and how do you consider ISO 31000 will circumvent those obstacles?
<--- Score

30. What communication problems can there be?
<--- Score

31. What kinds of problems/issues do they encounter?
<--- Score

32. Who needs to know or be involved?
<--- Score

33. Does your organization have a history of liquidity problems?
<--- Score

34. How capable are you of responding to events beyond your control that may happen in the future?
<--- Score

35. What problems occurred during and after the implementation of the model?
<--- Score

36. Do you have key management policies binding keys to identifiable owners?
<--- Score

37. What does your organization use and need in order to maintain identity service?
<--- Score

38. What specialized emergency information is needed by people with various disabilities in an emergency?
<--- Score

39. Do you need homegrown information models in enterprise architectures?

<--- Score

40. Who does or can influence this partnership, program, project or event?
<--- Score

41. Should substantive testing be an equally important element of an auditors identification of deficiencies in the control environment?
<--- Score

42. What does ISO 31000 success mean to the stakeholders?
<--- Score

43. What would happen if ISO 31000 weren't done?
<--- Score

44. How frequently does the information need to be collected?
<--- Score

Add up total points for this section:
_____ = Total points for this section

Divided by: ______ (number of statements answered) = ______ Average score for this section

Transfer your score to the ISO 31000 Index at the beginning of the Self-Assessment.

CRITERION #2: DEFINE:

INTENT: Formulate the stakeholder problem. Define the problem, needs and objectives.

In my belief, the answer to this question is clearly defined:

5 Strongly Agree

4 Agree

3 Neutral

2 Disagree

1 Strongly Disagree

1. Is the ISO 31000 scope manageable?
<--- Score

2. Is a person or entity your organization associate and required to enter into a written business associate contract?
<--- Score

3. Has the ISO 31000 work been fairly and/or equitably

divided and delegated among team members who are qualified and capable to perform the work? Has everyone contributed?
<--- Score

4. Is there a completed, verified, and validated high-level 'as is' (not 'should be' or 'could be') stakeholder process map?
<--- Score

5. Who are the ISO 31000 improvement team members, including Management Leads and Coaches?
<--- Score

6. Are there different segments of customers?
<--- Score

7. What are the Roles and Responsibilities for each team member and its leadership? Where is this documented?
<--- Score

8. Is ISO 31000 linked to key stakeholder goals and objectives?
<--- Score

9. What key stakeholder process output measure(s) does ISO 31000 leverage and how?
<--- Score

10. What resources are required?
<--- Score

11. Is there a critical path to deliver ISO 31000 results?
<--- Score

12. How is the team tracking and documenting its work?
<--- Score

13. Has a high-level 'as is' process map been completed, verified and validated?
<--- Score

14. What are the compelling stakeholder reasons for embarking on ISO 31000?
<--- Score

15. Will team members perform ISO 31000 work when assigned and in a timely fashion?
<--- Score

16. What are the dynamics of the communication plan?
<--- Score

17. What customer feedback methods were used to solicit their input?
<--- Score

18. Does the project require complicated or large amounts of security from the contractor(s)?
<--- Score

19. Did you examine your organizations internal context?
<--- Score

20. How did the ISO 31000 manager receive input to the development of a ISO 31000 improvement plan and the estimated completion dates/times of each

activity?
<--- Score

21. What would be the goal or target for a ISO 31000's improvement team?
<--- Score

22. Is a fully trained team formed, supported, and committed to work on the ISO 31000 improvements?
<--- Score

23. Which resources and capital allocations are required to implement the strategy?
<--- Score

24. Is there a ISO 31000 management charter, including stakeholder case, problem and goal statements, scope, milestones, roles and responsibilities, communication plan?
<--- Score

25. Are improvement team members fully trained on ISO 31000?
<--- Score

26. How many cases have been resolved?
<--- Score

27. Do the problem and goal statements meet the SMART criteria (specific, measurable, attainable, relevant, and time-bound)?
<--- Score

28. Has the improvement team collected the 'voice of the customer' (obtained feedback – qualitative and quantitative)?

<--- Score

29. Which options are the MOST relevant to assist in defining the Context?
<--- Score

30. What constraints exist that might impact the team?
<--- Score

31. How often are the team meetings?
<--- Score

32. Has a project plan, Gantt chart, or similar been developed/completed?
<--- Score

33. Are customer(s) identified and segmented according to their different needs and requirements?
<--- Score

34. Is the team formed and are team leaders (Coaches and Management Leads) assigned?
<--- Score

35. Has a team charter been developed and communicated?
<--- Score

36. When is/was the ISO 31000 start date?
<--- Score

37. Are stakeholder processes mapped?
<--- Score

38. Has anyone else (internal or external to the group)

attempted to solve this problem or a similar one before? If so, what knowledge can be leveraged from these previous efforts?
<--- Score

39. Have the customer needs been translated into specific, measurable requirements? How?
<--- Score

40. What are contextual differences of IT Governance in organizations and collaborative networks?
<--- Score

41. When are meeting minutes sent out? Who is on the distribution list?
<--- Score

42. When is the estimated completion date?
<--- Score

43. Realistic in terms of budget, scope and schedule?
<--- Score

44. Are you up to date with your reporting and compliance requirements?
<--- Score

45. Are customers identified and high impact areas defined?
<--- Score

46. Has the direction changed at all during the course of ISO 31000? If so, when did it change and why?
<--- Score

47. What specifically is the problem? Where does it occur? When does it occur? What is its extent?
<--- Score

48. Are team charters developed?
<--- Score

49. Are there any constraints known that bear on the ability to perform ISO 31000 work? How is the team addressing them?
<--- Score

50. Is the improvement team aware of the different versions of a process: what they think it is vs. what it actually is vs. what it should be vs. what it could be?
<--- Score

51. Has everyone on the team, including the team leaders, been properly trained?
<--- Score

52. How do you keep key subject matter experts in the loop?
<--- Score

53. Is the team adequately staffed with the desired cross-functionality? If not, what additional resources are available to the team?
<--- Score

54. Has/have the customer(s) been identified?
<--- Score

55. What critical content must be communicated – who, what, when, where, and how?

<--- Score

56. Does the team have regular meetings?
<--- Score

57. Is the current 'as is' process being followed? If not, what are the discrepancies?
<--- Score

58. What are the rough order estimates on cost savings/opportunities that ISO 31000 brings?
<--- Score

59. Is the team equipped with available and reliable resources?
<--- Score

60. Are different versions of process maps needed to account for the different types of inputs?
<--- Score

61. Is the team sponsored by a champion or stakeholder leader?
<--- Score

62. What are the boundaries of the scope? What is in bounds and what is not? What is the start point? What is the stop point?
<--- Score

63. Is there a completed SIPOC representation, describing the Suppliers, Inputs, Process, Outputs, and Customers?
<--- Score

64. How will variation in the actual durations of each

activity be dealt with to ensure that the expected ISO 31000 results are met?
<--- Score

65. Does the scope include an assessment of internal policies and procedures?
<--- Score

66. Will team members regularly document their ISO 31000 work?
<--- Score

67. Is ISO 31000 currently on schedule according to the plan?
<--- Score

68. How was the 'as is' process map developed, reviewed, verified and validated?
<--- Score

69. Are each of the mitigation tasks part of the in-scope work?
<--- Score

70. If substitutes have been appointed, have they been briefed on the ISO 31000 goals and received regular communications as to the progress to date?
<--- Score

71. Is data collected and displayed to better understand customer(s) critical needs and requirements.
<--- Score

72. Is full participation by members in regularly held team meetings guaranteed?

<--- Score

73. Is there regularly 100% attendance at the team meetings? If not, have appointed substitutes attended to preserve cross-functionality and full representation?
<--- Score

74. How will the ISO 31000 team and the group measure complete success of ISO 31000?
<--- Score

75. How does the ISO 31000 manager ensure against scope creep?
<--- Score

Add up total points for this section:
_____ = Total points for this section

Divided by: ______ (number of statements answered) = ______ Average score for this section

Transfer your score to the ISO 31000 Index at the beginning of the Self-Assessment.

CRITERION #3: MEASURE:

INTENT: Gather the correct data. Measure the current performance and evolution of the situation.

In my belief, the answer to this question is clearly defined:

5 Strongly Agree

4 Agree

3 Neutral

2 Disagree

1 Strongly Disagree

1. Is data collected on key measures that were identified?
<--- Score

2. What key measures identified indicate the performance of the stakeholder process?
<--- Score

3. What is the suitability of impact measurement

tools for determining the relative magnitude of sustainability risk relative to all other risks?
<--- Score

4. Why and what type of risk assessment is required - What criteria will you use to analyze risk?
<--- Score

5. Are enterprises examining enough of factors to calculate an accurate TCO, and in turn considering all the measures that can reduce costs and mitigate risks?
<--- Score

6. Is there a Performance Baseline?
<--- Score

7. Have you found any 'ground fruit' or 'low-hanging fruit' for immediate remedies to the gap in performance?
<--- Score

8. Where do your ERM efforts currently focus and how closely does it align to value creation, realization and preservation?
<--- Score

9. Does your organization analyze required capital?
<--- Score

10. How do you prioritize risks?
<--- Score

11. What is the significance of the risk in terms of

cost to the enterprise?
<--- Score

12. How much does third-party risk management cost?
<--- Score

13. Who could be impacted by the occurrence of the risk event?
<--- Score

14. What charts has the team used to display the components of variation in the process?
<--- Score

15. What are the financial measures that are the most important to management and board?
<--- Score

16. What are the key input variables? What are the key process variables? What are the key output variables?
<--- Score

17. If the identified risks were to occur, what is the impact it would have on the teams ability to produce or maintain the deliverable?
<--- Score

18. Who participated in the data collection for measurements?
<--- Score

19. Was a data collection plan established?
<--- Score

20. What are the agreed upon definitions of the high

impact areas, defect(s), unit(s), and opportunities that will figure into the process capability metrics?
<--- Score

21. Have impact areas been identified, as reputation, financial health, and regulatory compliance?
<--- Score

22. Is performance measurement and management fit for the future?
<--- Score

23. Initial and on-going risk analysis - do you regularly receive a threat assessment from outside experts?
<--- Score

24. Does your organization use enterprise risk management tools and/or processes to identify risks and opportunities and assess potential impact?
<--- Score

25. Where does the largest cost and risk exist?
<--- Score

26. What has the team done to assure the stability and accuracy of the measurement process?
<--- Score

27. Is a solid data collection plan established that includes measurement systems analysis?
<--- Score

28. Has management identified the right

categories of risk to focus on?
<--- Score

29. Where is risk the likely to impact?
<--- Score

30. Are process variation components displayed/ communicated using suitable charts, graphs, plots?
<--- Score

31. What are the objectives for voice analytics?
<--- Score

32. What external changes can impact your risk?
<--- Score

33. If a risk were to occur, what is the impact it would have on the teams ability to produce or maintain the deliverable?
<--- Score

34. How might the emergence of a global risk or megatrend impact your organizations strategy and operations?
<--- Score

35. What data was collected (past, present, future/ ongoing)?
<--- Score

36. Is data collection planned and executed?
<--- Score

37. How does a risk impact your organizations ability to achieve its strategy and business objectives?

<--- Score

38. Is this the lowest cost set of controls given your risk tolerance?
<--- Score

39. Is there potential for this project to be impacted by community or lobby groups?
<--- Score

40. Is it appropriate to allocate reinsurance costs proportional to risk?
<--- Score

41. Where is the risk likely to impact?
<--- Score

42. What is the value of a risk management focus?
<--- Score

43. What is the potential impact of the risk event?
<--- Score

44. Describe the nature of costs?
<--- Score

45. What will you do to ensure continued organizational focus on enterprise risk management?
<--- Score

46. Does the prioritization of risks align with risk appetite?
<--- Score

47. Has the responsible entity considered the

impact of all relevant legislation?
<--- Score

48. How do you measure it?
<--- Score

49. What platforms are you unable to measure accurately, or able to provide only limited measurements from?
<--- Score

50. How large is the gap between current performance and the customer-specified (goal) performance?
<--- Score

51. Is Process Variation Displayed/Communicated?
<--- Score

52. Is it understood that the risk management effectiveness critically depends on data collection, analysis and dissemination of relevant data?
<--- Score

53. Where should you focus?
<--- Score

54. How do you assess, prioritize and manage enterprise-wide talent risk?
<--- Score

55. Is long term and short term variability accounted for?
<--- Score

56. Is key measure data collection planned

and executed, process variation displayed and communicated and performance baselined?
<--- Score

57. Could you eliminate some controls and still have an acceptable residual risk level at a lower overall cost?
<--- Score

58. Is there a specific timetable for the initial risk identification and prioritization process?
<--- Score

59. Do you review the initial budgets and identify areas of possible cost reductions?
<--- Score

60. What will be the impact on your resources, processes, materials, finished products, vendors, customers, and most importantly regulatory compliance?
<--- Score

61. Are high impact defects defined and identified in the stakeholder process?
<--- Score

62. Are key measures identified and agreed upon?
<--- Score

63. What particular quality tools did the team find helpful in establishing measurements?
<--- Score

64. Will it help the enterprise to lower costs, improve process and better manage security risks?

<--- Score

65. What are the costs and benefits of managing the risk?
<--- Score

Add up total points for this section:
_____ = Total points for this section

Divided by: ______ (number of statements answered) = ______ Average score for this section

Transfer your score to the ISO 31000 Index at the beginning of the Self-Assessment.

CRITERION #4: ANALYZE:

INTENT: Analyze causes, assumptions and hypotheses.

In my belief, the answer to this question is clearly defined:

5 Strongly Agree

4 Agree

3 Neutral

2 Disagree

1 Strongly Disagree

1. Could the data-item make a difference to the category of decision?
<--- Score

2. Did you consider your governance as you design your process?
<--- Score

3. What did the team gain from developing a sub-process map?

<--- Score

4. How is internal audit involved in the risk management process?
<--- Score

5. Are gaps between current performance and the goal performance identified?
<--- Score

6. Are the application host process shut-down options acceptable?
<--- Score

7. Is the ISO 31000 process severely broken such that a re-design is necessary?
<--- Score

8. In creating an agile and flexible governance model, does your organization link its risk management practices to value drivers?
<--- Score

9. Are there appropriate channels and means to communicate and process information?
<--- Score

10. Is there an effective process for reliable reporting on risks and risk management performance?
<--- Score

11. What are the revised rough estimates of the financial savings/opportunity for ISO 31000 improvements?
<--- Score

12. What competencies are important to your organizations risk management process, and what type of training does your organization provide?
<--- Score

13. What tools were used to narrow the list of possible causes?
<--- Score

14. Who owns this process in your organization?
<--- Score

15. What work has been done internally to establish an ERM process?
<--- Score

16. Is well-managed risk taking encouraged to help seize opportunities and support effective innovation?
<--- Score

17. What tools were used to generate the list of possible causes?
<--- Score

18. Does the data apply to the defined scope of the risk?
<--- Score

19. Have the problem and goal statements been updated to reflect the additional knowledge gained from the analyze phase?
<--- Score

20. Have there been any significant changes

to your organizations IT systems (changes in hardware, software, processes or personnel)?
<--- Score

21. How was the detailed process map generated, verified, and validated?
<--- Score

22. Is there a vigorous process for the development and implementation of compliance training?
<--- Score

23. Have any additional benefits been identified that will result from closing all or most of the gaps?
<--- Score

24. How can an enterprise approach to risk and opportunity management make a real difference to the bottom line?
<--- Score

25. Was a detailed process map created to amplify critical steps of the 'as is' stakeholder process?
<--- Score

26. Is there a cohesive compliance process?
<--- Score

27. Did any value-added analysis or 'lean thinking' take place to identify some of the gaps shown on the 'as is' process map?
<--- Score

28. Have you included regular checks or surveillance in your risk processes at all levels?

<--- Score

29. Is there an opportunity for outside departments to assert control or interference?
<--- Score

30. Is there a process to update policies and procedures?
<--- Score

31. Is the board satisfied that the strategy-setting process appropriately considers a substantive assessment of the risks the enterprise is assuming as a result of the strategy selected?
<--- Score

32. Do the results of the security categorization process reflect your organizations risk management strategy?
<--- Score

33. Who is leading the Risk process and how is the procedure?
<--- Score

34. Where are opportunities within your organization to improve risk management?
<--- Score

35. Are all strategies and solutions reviewed for value-creation opportunities?
<--- Score

36. Where is sensitive data created and stored outside of your enterprise?
<--- Score

37. How would you be harmed if the information/ data were unexpectedly changed?
<--- Score

38. Is data and process analysis, root cause analysis and quantifying the gap/opportunity in place?
<--- Score

39. How much data should be collected and how much information should be shared?
<--- Score

40. What is your level of concern with respect to the overall risk management capability of your area of responsibility to seize opportunities and manage risks?
<--- Score

41. What level of integration with business processes have you achieved in your approach to content and records management?
<--- Score

42. Who should participate during the risk assessment process?
<--- Score

43. What quality tools were used to get through the analyze phase?
<--- Score

44. Which controls and business processes are in place to address this risk?
<--- Score

45. How can data lead to better corporate governance?
<--- Score

46. What were the financial benefits resulting from any 'ground fruit or low-hanging fruit' (quick fixes)?
<--- Score

47. Were there any improvement opportunities identified from the process analysis?
<--- Score

48. Were Pareto charts (or similar) used to portray the 'heavy hitters' (or key sources of variation)?
<--- Score

49. Has the enterprise appropriately identified significant areas of potential risk resulting from the related processes?
<--- Score

50. What tasks are new work that should be addressed through the IV&V budget processes?
<--- Score

51. Is there a certification process?
<--- Score

52. How what is the risks faced, and what are the applied enterprise risk management processes used to deal with the already stated risks?
<--- Score

53. What competencies are important to the organizations risk management process, and what type of training does the organization provide?

<--- Score

54. What is the enterprise strategy for data security?
<--- Score

55. What data elements are needed in the risk management system?
<--- Score

56. Has management conducted a comprehensive evaluation of the entirety of enterprise Risk Management at least once every three years or sooner if a major strategy or management change occurs, a program is added or deleted, changes in economic or political conditions exist, or changes in operations or methods of processing information have occurred?
<--- Score

57. What is the cost of poor quality as supported by the team's analysis?
<--- Score

58. Do you have a clearly defined organizational structure at organization level in order to sustain the risk management process?
<--- Score

59. Are there incentives to drive employee behavior to implement the strategies?
<--- Score

60. How do you convince the line of the value of risk management and drive change?
<--- Score

61. Who should you get involved in the definition of your enterprise approach and what should roles be in the risk identification and risk management process?
<--- Score

62. Do your data management policies and procedures address tenant and service level conflicts of interests?
<--- Score

63. Did any additional data need to be collected?
<--- Score

64. How is the budget integrated with the overall enterprise risk management process?
<--- Score

65. Do you think your current change management processes put you at risk of a security breach?
<--- Score

66. What are the significant risks top management is willing to take and the opportunities it is willing to pursue?
<--- Score

67. Is the performance gap determined?
<--- Score

68. Are response processes and procedures executable and are they being maintained?
<--- Score

69. Is the gap/opportunity displayed and communicated in financial terms?
<--- Score

70. Was a cause-and-effect diagram used to explore the different types of causes (or sources of variation)?
<--- Score

71. What trends and events will drive new business investment in IT?
<--- Score

72. What conclusions were drawn from the team's data collection and analysis? How did the team reach these conclusions?
<--- Score

73. Does your process for third party due diligence and risk management correspond to enterprise risk associated with the activity?
<--- Score

74. What information is needed to support the Business Process?
<--- Score

75. Are you also forced to address significant risk and uncertainty with incumbent market data vendors?
<--- Score

76. What were the crucial 'moments of truth' on the process map?
<--- Score

77. How much data is the right amount of data to

collect?
<--- Score

78. What are the common mistakes and pitfalls during the risk assessment process?
<--- Score

79. Which communication-driven risk incidents related to poor communications is your enterprise most concerned about?
<--- Score

80. What does the data say about the performance of the stakeholder process?
<--- Score

81. How effective are your existing control processes?
<--- Score

82. Were any designed experiments used to generate additional insight into the data analysis?
<--- Score

83. Where might you look to identify what asset management tools and processes are available?
<--- Score

84. Do you have data that show is that organizations adopting ERM improve financial performance relative to past performance and after controlling, for industry performance?
<--- Score

Add up total points for this section:
_____ = Total points for this section

Divided by: ______ (number of statements answered) = ______ Average score for this section

Transfer your score to the ISO 31000 Index at the beginning of the Self-Assessment.

CRITERION #5: IMPROVE:

INTENT: Develop a practical solution. Innovate, establish and test the solution and to measure the results.

In my belief, the answer to this question is clearly defined:

5 Strongly Agree

4 Agree

3 Neutral

2 Disagree

1 Strongly Disagree

1. Do the risk management initiatives generate value for organization?
<--- Score

2. Are you effectively carrying out your responsibilities as a board in overseeing risk management?
<--- Score

3. Why do departments adopt risk management initiatives?
<--- Score

4. What corporate strategy or strategies does this risk relate to?
<--- Score

5. Have entities met the requirements of cyber security risk management framework?
<--- Score

6. What dollar range best describes your organizations annual enterprise risk management automation (products and services) in the upcoming fiscal year?
<--- Score

7. Is the venture promising you high rates of return for little or no financial risk?
<--- Score

8. Is there a senior champion for risk management in your organization?
<--- Score

9. What are the common security or risk-related concerns?
<--- Score

10. What are the current behaviors that contribute or detract from achieving the desired risk culture?
<--- Score

11. Has the risk terminology/language been agreed?

<--- Score

12. Why do environmental, social and governance-related risks matter for business?
<--- Score

13. Did you think about how risk management should be applied?
<--- Score

14. Does your organization have the skills and experience to effectively manage risk?
<--- Score

15. How do you integrate strategy and risk management?
<--- Score

16. Is supply chain risk management integrated into your enterprise risk management approach?
<--- Score

17. Is the risk function covering the proper portion of the enterprise with detailed risk assessments?
<--- Score

18. How do you encourage a culture of risk management at the operational r level?
<--- Score

19. What steps has top management taken to ensure oversight over the management of the risks?
<--- Score

20. What challenges face risk managers today?

<--- Score

21. What tools and technologies does your organization leverage to make informed decisions about its third-party relationships?
<--- Score

22. Why is this omission a serious inhibitor in conversations - let alone negotiations - about risk?
<--- Score

23. What are the fundamental considerations in changing the risk culture?
<--- Score

24. How do you overcome this risk aversion?
<--- Score

25. Is there an incumbent organization that has provided risk management, audit or other related consulting services?
<--- Score

26. Did you think about what kind of risk management methods will be needed?
<--- Score

27. What level of importance does the Board ascribe to enterprise risk management?
<--- Score

28. How are supply chain risk assessments and risk management strategies communicated throughout the enterprise?
<--- Score

29. What kind of a financial risk management strategy would you create to solve the already stated issues?
<--- Score

30. How good is your organizations board / executive management at getting assurance on the performance of IT and on the mitigation of IT risks?
<--- Score

31. How does your organization make risk tolerance useful in managing risk?
<--- Score

32. How are the board and the management team involved in risk management?
<--- Score

33. Do entities have a fit for purpose cyber security risk management framework?
<--- Score

34. Why is risk management culture important?
<--- Score

35. What is risk management in procurement?
<--- Score

36. Are the outcomes of risk management able to be effectively measured?
<--- Score

37. How is risk management viewed at your organization along continuum?
<--- Score

38. How can organizations advance from good IT Risk Management practice to great?
<--- Score

39. Does interest rate risk affect investments in property-casualty insurance stocks?
<--- Score

40. Does your enterprise manage this level of risk?
<--- Score

41. What are the benefits of risk management?
<--- Score

42. What are the main features of your organizations risk culture in terms of tone at the top?
<--- Score

43. Will the risks defined in the risk appetite determination relevant to the r overall level of risk?
<--- Score

44. What additional risk treatment is required?
<--- Score

45. How capable is your organization of managing risk?
<--- Score

46. Does a culture exist that supports an enterprise-wide risk philosophy?
<--- Score

47. Is risk management performance embedded in recruitment and performance appraisal?
<--- Score

48. Did your organization take enough risk to attain its target?
<--- Score

49. What platform will you use to stratify clients according to risk across all settings?
<--- Score

50. Is your organization taking sufficient risk to attain its target?
<--- Score

51. Did you think about where risk management should be applied?
<--- Score

52. How do you capture this risk information?
<--- Score

53. Does it include risk assessments for third parties?
<--- Score

54. Is enterprise risk management a similar fad that will pass soon?
<--- Score

55. Are the risks associated with working with other organizations assessed and managed?
<--- Score

56. How do enterprises organize and staff supply

chain risk management organizations?
<--- Score

57. Is the compliance register linked to the risk register?
<--- Score

58. How do you control the risks so that harm is unlikely?
<--- Score

59. What specific factors should the risk appetite take into account in terms of the business context?
<--- Score

60. What is the perspective of existing Risk information, who is getting it?
<--- Score

61. Has senior management provided guidelines for the Enterprises risk/return expectations?
<--- Score

62. How effective is your organization at mitigating risk?
<--- Score

63. What exactly is meant by enterprise risk management?
<--- Score

64. Does any organization specifically identify reputation risk?
<--- Score

65. Did you specify the scope of your risk

management activities?
<--- Score

66. What is risk and risk management?
<--- Score

67. How much risk does your organization take?
<--- Score

68. What does risk management have to do?
<--- Score

69. What is the latest in enterprise risk management?
<--- Score

70. How to establish risk tolerance?
<--- Score

71. What is wrong with risk matrices?
<--- Score

72. Does the group have a publicly available Risk Management policy?
<--- Score

73. Are you adequately preparing your employees for assuming risk ownership responsibilities?
<--- Score

74. How much of each risk type will you take on?
<--- Score

75. Is it the same as gross risk or residual risk ?
<--- Score

76. Does management lead by example and display leadership, especially regarding risk management?
<--- Score

77. Why mobile devices could be risky?
<--- Score

78. Did you think about what risk management should include?
<--- Score

79. Can highly-effective IT Risk Management programs ever eliminate IT Risk?
<--- Score

80. How is enterprise risk management helping to inform your strategic direction?
<--- Score

81. Is risk management mentioned in any report?
<--- Score

82. Did you think about how your internal context could influence risk management?
<--- Score

83. What is meant by an acceptable level of risk?
<--- Score

84. Are risks managed to ensure some are within your organizations risk appetite?
<--- Score

85. Has the risk of a residual market assessment been considered in the Filing?

<--- Score

86. Do risk owners, sustainability managers and risk managers collaborate on a regular basis?
<--- Score

87. Where does risk management reside?
<--- Score

88. What knowledge and skill is needed for the already stated who make decisions to make risk management a part of decision making?
<--- Score

89. Are organizations hiring savvy, cybersecurity leaders with risk management experience?
<--- Score

90. What possible threats put your business assets at risk ?
<--- Score

91. How do you ensure effective risk management is used across the enterprise?
<--- Score

92. How does your organization build its capabilities for IT Risk Management?
<--- Score

93. Do you have an effective risk policy?
<--- Score

94. Is your nursing home certification at risk?
<--- Score

95. Do you consider risks and risk management issues with external stakeholders?
<--- Score

96. How do you decide what problems to address?
<--- Score

97. Did you think about what kind of risk assessment tools will be needed?
<--- Score

98. What type of insurance or other risk-management services do you need?
<--- Score

99. Is there a right structure for risk management?
<--- Score

100. Is corrective action taken to address excessive risks?
<--- Score

101. Are there any actions in progress to deal with risk?
<--- Score

102. Why is setting risk tolerance important?
<--- Score

103. What is the nature of the risk and the action required?
<--- Score

104. How are risks and issues organized; can it fit with what management sees?
<--- Score

105. How could the key principles of risk management be fed into in the work of regulatory stakeholders?
<--- Score

106. Are procuring entity decisions subject to appeal to the judicial branch?
<--- Score

107. How much time is devoted to risk assessment?
<--- Score

108. How do you encourage a culture of risk management at the operational level?
<--- Score

109. How do current investments, operations and commitments compare to your organizations risk appetite?
<--- Score

110. What controls are already in place to address this risk?
<--- Score

111. How significant is your organizations commitment to enterprise risk management?
<--- Score

112. Does the existing structure allow for an enterprise-wide view of risk management?
<--- Score

113. How is this linked to the expectations of Risk

Management?
<--- Score

114. What is possible with a strong risk culture?
<--- Score

115. Will it make the job of risk management easier or simpler?
<--- Score

116. How can the risk manager ensure the right risks are taken for your organization?
<--- Score

117. What business benefits can be achieved by adopting an effective Enterprise Risk Management programme?
<--- Score

118. Is the risk register kept up to date?
<--- Score

119. Does relying on criticality put your organization at risk?
<--- Score

120. What is strategic risk management?
<--- Score

121. Is the risk management function concentrated in any particular department or business unit?
<--- Score

122. When and how does senior management report risk information to you?

<--- Score

123. Do employees feel accountable for the proper application of risk policies and take ownership for your organizations risk strategy?
<--- Score

124. Is there a general culture of risk management at all levels?
<--- Score

125. Why does reputation rarely feature on the risk register?
<--- Score

126. Does the enterprise employ an effective risk-based approach to strategic decisions?
<--- Score

127. What is risk management (and its alternative title enterprise risk management)?
<--- Score

128. Has management identified strategic risks?
<--- Score

129. Is it important that internal audit annually reviews your organizations risk management function?
<--- Score

130. How is risk management handled in scrum teams compared to previous waterfall method?
<--- Score

Add up total points for this section:

_____ = Total points for this section

Divided by: ______ (number of statements answered) = ______ Average score for this section

Transfer your score to the ISO 31000 Index at the beginning of the Self-Assessment.

CRITERION #6: CONTROL:

INTENT: Implement the practical solution. Maintain the performance and correct possible complications.

In my belief, the answer to this question is clearly defined:

5 Strongly Agree

4 Agree

3 Neutral

2 Disagree

1 Strongly Disagree

1. Did you plan how to make this process an integral part of your organizations projects?
<--- Score

2. Are suggested corrective/restorative actions indicated on the response plan for known causes to problems that might surface?
<--- Score

3. Is reporting being used or needed?
<--- Score

4. How will report readings be checked to effectively monitor performance?
<--- Score

5. Do you have a plan in place for reputation management after an event?
<--- Score

6. Does the treatment plan identify priority order for risk treatments?
<--- Score

7. Have all the principles under the ERM component monitoring been considered?
<--- Score

8. Do all purchase orders comply with authorized payment and delivery expectation standard terms?
<--- Score

9. Do you continually improve the risk policy, framework, plans?
<--- Score

10. Are experts willing to assist in the development of corresponding standards?
<--- Score

11. Does management have a process for monitoring project schedules?
<--- Score

12. What are the available guides and standards to plan and conduct and document the independent reviews?
<--- Score

13. Are new process steps, standards, and documentation ingrained into normal operations?
<--- Score

14. Is there procedures for employees, management to report internal control weaknesses?
<--- Score

15. Do you have a Risk Management Plan?
<--- Score

16. How do you learn from virtual team snapshots that can help inform new organizational forms?
<--- Score

17. Is there a comprehensive Risk Management Plan in place?
<--- Score

18. Do you employ access controls on customer information systems?
<--- Score

19. Are key risk indicators monitored during strategic execution?
<--- Score

20. Will you provide a copy of the current mission and vision statements, and portions of the strategic plan or objective related to this ERM

project? If so please attach them to the response
<--- Score

21. Is there a documented and implemented monitoring plan?
<--- Score

22. What differentiates ISO 31000 from other standards?
<--- Score

23. Is there a recommended audit plan for routine surveillance inspections of ISO 31000's gains?
<--- Score

24. What is an international standard?
<--- Score

25. What about the risk management theme in other generic management system standards?
<--- Score

26. Why is this standard a good idea?
<--- Score

27. Is there a transfer of ownership and knowledge to process owner and process team tasked with the responsibilities.
<--- Score

28. How familiar are you with how international standards are developed through ISO, the International Organization for Standardization?
<--- Score

29. Is the data collected in accordance with a time-

tested or industry standard?
<--- Score

30. What other adjustments must be made to the loss adjustment expense factor in order to use it?
<--- Score

31. Who among the management team is monitoring the already stated signals?
<--- Score

32. Is there a control plan in place for sustaining improvements (short and long-term)?
<--- Score

33. What would you expect to see in the first year risk management transformation plan?
<--- Score

34. What is the control/monitoring plan?
<--- Score

35. Do you enforce access control policies and protect sensitive information through effective management of enterprise entitlements?
<--- Score

36. What is an asset management plan?
<--- Score

37. Are documented procedures clear and easy to follow for the operators?
<--- Score

38. What quality tools were useful in the control phase?

<--- Score

39. What else do you need to learn to be ready?
<--- Score

40. What is the recommended frequency of auditing?
<--- Score

41. Do you have monitoring systems in the potential high risk areas that identify the changing of risk level?
<--- Score

42. Do you restrict, log and monitor access to your information security management systems?
<--- Score

43. Are there arrangements for agreed standards for assessing risks?
<--- Score

44. Has the improved process and its steps been standardized?
<--- Score

45. How will the day-to-day responsibilities for monitoring and continual improvement be transferred from the improvement team to the process owner?
<--- Score

46. Does a troubleshooting guide exist or is it needed?
<--- Score

47. Are there are any problems related to poor planning?

<--- Score

48. What is the relative importance of the control and is the overall control objective achieved by interaction with other control activities and mitigating factors?
<--- Score

49. How effective are controls (barriers)?
<--- Score

50. Do your recovery plans incorporate lessons learned?
<--- Score

51. Does management have access to a robust set of key risk indicators to monitor its top risks?
<--- Score

52. What are documentation standards?
<--- Score

53. What assumptions are integral to your organizations strategic plan?
<--- Score

54. Do you know what your expected returns are, as adjusted for risk?
<--- Score

55. Who is the ISO 31000 process owner?
<--- Score

56. How will new or emerging customer needs/ requirements be checked/communicated to orient the process toward meeting the new specifications

and continually reducing variation?
<--- Score

57. How will the process owner and team be able to hold the gains?
<--- Score

58. Is a response plan established and deployed?
<--- Score

59. What makes this different from the internal control framework?
<--- Score

60. What other areas of the group might benefit from the ISO 31000 team's improvements, knowledge, and learning?
<--- Score

61. Are there documented procedures?
<--- Score

62. How will input, process, and output variables be checked to detect for sub-optimal conditions?
<--- Score

63. Did you plan how to make this process an integral part of your organizations programs?
<--- Score

64. Is a response plan in place for when the input, process, or output measures indicate an 'out-of-control' condition?
<--- Score

65. How are standards or guidelines utilized

by organizations in the implementation of corresponding practices?
<--- Score

66. How will the process owner verify improvement in present and future sigma levels, process capabilities?
<--- Score

67. Will a permanent standard be developed?
<--- Score

68. How well tested is the continuity plan for this project?
<--- Score

69. How might the group capture best practices and lessons learned so as to leverage improvements?
<--- Score

70. Which industry standard for risk management does your Department or organization predominately follow?
<--- Score

71. What are the critical parameters to watch?
<--- Score

72. Do you have and implement a strategic plan?
<--- Score

73. What about the Compliance / Control aspects?
<--- Score

74. Do you ensure enterprise user account access is effectively logged to aid in the real-time monitoring and alerting of excess privilege, policy

violations, and anomalous behavior?
<--- Score

75. What is the existing Enterprise Risk Management framework in your organization to identify, prioritize, mitigate and monitor risks?
<--- Score

76. Is the plan for managing operational risk communicated to stakeholders?
<--- Score

77. Does the response plan contain a definite closed loop continual improvement scheme (e.g., plan-do-check-act)?
<--- Score

78. How do you adjust your processes to better fit risk management?
<--- Score

79. How do you keep them under control?
<--- Score

80. Do risk management leaders and the already stated leading the strategic planning process interact frequently?
<--- Score

81. Who plans to (or is in the process) of implementing ISO 31000?
<--- Score

82. Is there documentation that will support the successful operation of the improvement?
<--- Score

83. What are the limitations that impede you to implement the risk mitigation plans?
<--- Score

84. Do you regularly monitor your risk status for early warning signs that changes are needed to your controls and/or objectives?
<--- Score

85. Will any special training be provided for results interpretation?
<--- Score

86. How does scrum framework employ risk management compared to standards and practices used today?
<--- Score

87. What key inputs and outputs are being measured on an ongoing basis?
<--- Score

88. What is your process/plan for managing risk?
<--- Score

89. Is knowledge gained on process shared and institutionalized?
<--- Score

90. Is your organization updating critical risk management documents based on ongoing monitoring activities?
<--- Score

91. How does payroll fit into your organizations

plan to implement a new information technology system?
<--- Score

92. Is new knowledge gained imbedded in the response plan?
<--- Score

93. What should the next improvement project be that is related to ISO 31000?
<--- Score

94. Has proper consideration been given to application controls and security?
<--- Score

95. Does job training on the documented procedures need to be part of the process team's education and training?
<--- Score

96. Is there a standardized process?
<--- Score

97. How do risk analysis and Risk Management inform your organizations decision making processes for long-range system planning, major project description and cost estimation, priority programming, and project development?
<--- Score

98. Does the mitigation plan contain interim steps to address this risk?
<--- Score

99. Have appropriate industry or other external

standards been applied?
<--- Score

100. Have new or revised work instructions resulted?
<--- Score

101. Does the internal control plan include information account foring how and when management monitors each ERM component in the plan?
<--- Score

102. Are operating procedures consistent?
<--- Score

103. Does the ISO 31000 performance meet the customer's requirements?
<--- Score

104. What other systems, operations, processes, and infrastructures (hiring practices, staffing, training, incentives/rewards, metrics/dashboards/scorecards, etc.) need updates, additions, changes, or deletions in order to facilitate knowledge transfer and improvements?
<--- Score

105. How will the standards be used?
<--- Score

106. Have the it security cost for all investments/ projects been integrated in to the overall cost including (certification and accreditation/ re-accreditation, system security plan, risk assessment, privacy impact assessment, configuration/patch management, security control

testing and evaluation, and contingency planning/ testing)?
<--- Score

Add up total points for this section:
_____ = Total points for this section

Divided by: ______ (number of statements answered) = ______ Average score for this section

Transfer your score to the ISO 31000 Index at the beginning of the Self-Assessment.

CRITERION #7: SUSTAIN:

INTENT: Retain the benefits.

In my belief, the answer to this question is clearly defined:

5 Strongly Agree

4 Agree

3 Neutral

2 Disagree

1 Strongly Disagree

1. What are the costs?
<--- Score

2. Why the need?
<--- Score

3. Are you trying to see the whole picture or just one small part?
<--- Score

4. How will the change process be managed?

<--- Score

5. What portion of your position is allocated to youth protection?
<--- Score

6. What are the clients issues and concerns?
<--- Score

7. What is your organizations process which leads to recognition of value generation?
<--- Score

8. What are the strengths and weaknesses of your business unit?
<--- Score

9. Pragmatically determine resources necessary to complete the objective. Are corresponding resources readily available?
<--- Score

10. Who are the users of the tools and technology?
<--- Score

11. Does your organizations product line cover the customers entire financial services experience?
<--- Score

12. What are predictive ISO 31000 analytics?
<--- Score

13. Where is training needed?
<--- Score

14. Is a written procedure or checklist in place to

do this?
<--- Score

15. Do you make product suggestions based on the customers order or purchase history?
<--- Score

16. Where are the boundaries of a field determined?
<--- Score

17. What ISO 31000 data should be managed?
<--- Score

18. What all changes do you think should be made in the way assessment is done as of now?
<--- Score

19. Who will facilitate the team and process?
<--- Score

20. How do you verify the ISO 31000 requirements quality?
<--- Score

21. How do you prevent mis-estimating cost?
<--- Score

22. Does the problem have ethical dimensions?
<--- Score

23. Who qualifies to gain access to data?
<--- Score

24. Why do other organizations hedge?
<--- Score

25. What is the amount of loss the enterprise wants to accept to pursue a return?
<--- Score

26. What must the ERM policy address?
<--- Score

27. Why is this needed?
<--- Score

28. Is there a well-articulated, even-handed, evenly enforced disciplinary policy?
<--- Score

29. What resources or support might you need?
<--- Score

30. Is the project teams time dedicated and adequate for this project?
<--- Score

31. Evidence of erm components - does it include all principles related to each component?
<--- Score

32. Who are the ISO 31000 decision-makers?
<--- Score

33. Where is the cost?
<--- Score

34. How are outputs preserved and protected?
<--- Score

35. Who gets your output?

<--- Score

36. Would you develop a ISO 31000 Communication Strategy?
<--- Score

37. What position has product management in the enterprise?
<--- Score

38. What are your organizations mission, vision, core values, strategy and business objectives?
<--- Score

39. How many input/output points does it require?
<--- Score

40. What adjustments to the strategies are needed?
<--- Score

41. What are the information security considerations in cloud computing?
<--- Score

42. What types of data do your ISO 31000 indicators require?
<--- Score

43. What qualifications are needed?
<--- Score

44. What qualifies as competition?
<--- Score

45. Has the board established a compliance policy?

<--- Score

46. ISO 31000 risk decisions: whose call Is It?
<--- Score

47. How do you ensure that the ISO 31000 opportunity is realistic?
<--- Score

48. What is the ISO 31000 problem definition? What do you need to resolve?
<--- Score

49. Is the scope clearly documented?
<--- Score

50. What is the definition of ISO 31000 excellence?
<--- Score

51. Are procedures documented for managing ISO 31000 risks?
<--- Score

52. What is your ISO 31000 quality cost segregation study?
<--- Score

53. What are your operating costs?
<--- Score

54. What information qualified as important?
<--- Score

55. Who manages ISO 31000 risk?
<--- Score

56. What are the affordable ISO 31000 risks?
<--- Score

57. What were the criteria for evaluating a ISO 31000 pilot?
<--- Score

58. What do employees need in the short term?
<--- Score

59. Is the project located within an operational or public area?
<--- Score

60. Where do you obtain additional information about workplace accommodations?
<--- Score

61. How will corresponding data be collected?
<--- Score

62. How will costs be allocated?
<--- Score

63. What is the extent or complexity of the ISO 31000 problem?
<--- Score

64. What technology is driving the third wave of threat intelligence in enterprises?
<--- Score

65. Who are the key stakeholders for the ISO 31000 evaluation?
<--- Score

66. Is there a master list of vendor relationships, with assurance each provides value?
<--- Score

67. How do you quantify and qualify impacts?
<--- Score

68. Are problem definition and motivation clearly presented?
<--- Score

69. How does operational effectiveness and efficiency build on compliance initiatives?
<--- Score

70. Are there regulatory / compliance issues?
<--- Score

71. Did management take appropriate action in response to consultant recommendations?
<--- Score

72. Why do other organizations migrate to enterprise systems?
<--- Score

73. Are all requirements met?
<--- Score

74. Why do other organizations care?
<--- Score

75. How do you manage unclear ISO 31000 requirements?
<--- Score

76. What are the ISO 31000 tasks and definitions?
<--- Score

77. What are your outputs?
<--- Score

78. What causes innovation to fail or succeed in your organization?
<--- Score

79. What are customers monitoring?
<--- Score

80. What ISO 31000 capabilities do you need?
<--- Score

81. Are events managed to resolution?
<--- Score

82. Where can you get qualified talent today?
<--- Score

83. What if you had cloud key management?
<--- Score

84. How are policy decisions made and where?
<--- Score

85. How are training requirements identified?
<--- Score

86. What is ISO 31000 risk?
<--- Score

87. How much value do you believe your organization has received in areas from its

program?
<--- Score

88. What are the ISO 31000 design outputs?
<--- Score

89. What ISO 31000 metrics are outputs of the process?
<--- Score

90. Have design-to-cost goals been established?
<--- Score

91. What causes investor action?
<--- Score

92. What change management practices does your organization employ?
<--- Score

93. How can you manage cost down?
<--- Score

94. Can visitors/customers opt out of sharing personal information?
<--- Score

95. What is your cost benefit analysis?
<--- Score

96. Who are your customers?
<--- Score

97. What should senior management and boards know?
<--- Score

98. How many open tickets are there?
<--- Score

99. What is the cause of any ISO 31000 gaps?
<--- Score

100. Are the ISO 31000 requirements complete?
<--- Score

101. Was a life-cycle cost analysis performed?
<--- Score

102. Have you identified breakpoints and/or risk tolerances that will trigger broad consideration of a potential need for intervention or modification of strategy?
<--- Score

103. Is ISO 31000 documentation maintained?
<--- Score

104. Do calls labeled Self Service speak to a CSR?
<--- Score

105. Is the user enabled and does the user have at least one security role?
<--- Score

106. How can you better manage risk?
<--- Score

107. Is scope creep really all bad news?
<--- Score

108. What are the key components of the COSO

ERM Framework you are using?
<--- Score

109. What, related to, ISO 31000 processes does your organization outsource?
<--- Score

110. Do you understand your management processes today?
<--- Score

111. How do you identify subcontractor relationships?
<--- Score

112. Whom do you really need or want to serve?
<--- Score

113. Is there a strict change management process?
<--- Score

114. Which information does the ISO 31000 business case need to include?
<--- Score

115. What does it mean to implement ERM ?
<--- Score

116. Does your organizations strengths be preserved?
<--- Score

117. What needs to stay?
<--- Score

118. Is there an established change management

process?
<--- Score

119. Do organizations experience a change in earnings volatility around ERM adoption?
<--- Score

120. How much do other organizations hedge with derivatives?
<--- Score

121. Is the e-mail tagging performance acceptable?
<--- Score

122. What are the processes for audit reporting and management?
<--- Score

123. Will the team be available to assist members in planning investigations?
<--- Score

124. Can you adapt and adjust to changing ISO 31000 situations?
<--- Score

125. What do you consider a short call and what is the threshold in seconds?
<--- Score

126. What details are required of the ISO 31000 cost structure?
<--- Score

127. What ISO 31000 problem should be solved?

<--- Score

128. Do you have separate key management and key usage duties?
<--- Score

129. Is there strong executive leadership commitment as demonstrated by communications, actions, budget (especially during tough economic times)?
<--- Score

130. Why does a customer first purchase your offering?
<--- Score

131. Do you need different information or graphics?
<--- Score

132. Do the viable solutions scale to future needs?
<--- Score

133. What is your perception of risk management and ISO 31000 globally?
<--- Score

134. How do you compare to other systems?
<--- Score

135. When are costs are incurred?
<--- Score

136. When a disaster occurs, who gets priority?
<--- Score

137. How does cost-to-serve analysis help?
<--- Score

138. Are supply costs steady or fluctuating?
<--- Score

139. What was the context?
<--- Score

140. How can a ISO 31000 test verify your ideas or assumptions?
<--- Score

141. What intelligence can you gather?
<--- Score

142. Which information should be logged?
<--- Score

143. Is the ISO 31000 solution sustainable?
<--- Score

144. Is risk periodically assessed?
<--- Score

145. What are the personnel training and qualifications required?
<--- Score

146. What capabilities do you have to implement corresponding actions?
<--- Score

147. What procurement laws and regulations apply to your organization?
<--- Score

148. What are you protecting?
<--- Score

149. How do you benefit from a ISO 31000 certification?
<--- Score

150. Are ISO 31000 vulnerabilities categorized and prioritized?
<--- Score

151. When you map the key players in your own work and the types/domains of relationships with them, which relationships do you find easy and which challenging, and why?
<--- Score

152. Which issues are too important to ignore?
<--- Score

153. How do you deal with ISO 31000 risk?
<--- Score

154. Have you ever wondered what happens to that barely used bar of soap in your hotel room?
<--- Score

155. What it systems do you have in your enterprise?
<--- Score

156. Are you able to realize any cost savings?
<--- Score

157. Is the ISO 31000 risk managed?

<--- Score

158. Is there executive leadership directing and accountable for telehealth services?
<--- Score

159. Is information provided in a clear and concise manner?
<--- Score

160. How do you catch ISO 31000 definition inconsistencies?
<--- Score

161. What is the cost of rework?
<--- Score

162. What qualifications are necessary?
<--- Score

163. Are the ISO 31000 benefits worth its costs?
<--- Score

164. What harm might be caused?
<--- Score

165. What are the information elements and structures involved in the KMS?
<--- Score

166. Are there employee screening/background checks?
<--- Score

167. The political context: who holds power?
<--- Score

168. What does your culture of compliance look like?
<--- Score

169. Is there any way to speed up the process?
<--- Score

170. What ISO 31000 data do you gather or use now?
<--- Score

171. What must you excel at?
<--- Score

172. What are the strategic priorities for this year?
<--- Score

173. How much does it cost?
<--- Score

174. Is key sustainability information integrated into existing reporting systems and/or ERP platforms?
<--- Score

175. What are the Biggest Challenges to the ERM Program at your organization?
<--- Score

176. How are collaborative networks implementing IT Governance?
<--- Score

177. How do you manage ISO 31000 risk?
<--- Score

178. What are the concrete ISO 31000 results?
<--- Score

179. How should your organization interpret ISO 31000 to develop and implement a risk management framework that is consistent with this standard?
<--- Score

180. What ISO 31000 coordination do you need?
<--- Score

181. What is the network quality, including speed and dropped packets?
<--- Score

182. What are internal audits recommendations for corrective action?
<--- Score

183. Is there any other ISO 31000 solution?
<--- Score

184. Do all implemented strategies have an assigned responsible party?
<--- Score

185. Does everyone receive the same training?
<--- Score

186. Is top management immediately told?
<--- Score

187. Why the management of risk should be based on ISO 31000?

<--- Score

188. How can risk management be tied procedurally to process elements?
<--- Score

189. What is the standard for acceptable ISO 31000 performance?
<--- Score

190. How much data can be collected in the given timeframe?
<--- Score

191. Is the position responsible for making significant recommendations due to expertise or knowledge?
<--- Score

192. Are there incentives for compliance as a job performance element/penalties for failure to perform?
<--- Score

193. When shipping a product, do you send tracking information to the customer?
<--- Score

194. How will the employee reporting the information be advised of conclusions and actions taken?
<--- Score

195. Is back end support per organization or enterprise wide?
<--- Score

196. Is there an opportunity to verify requirements?
<--- Score

197. What gets examined?
<--- Score

198. What independent validation and compliance functions are there?
<--- Score

199. Are the risks fully understood, reasonable and manageable?
<--- Score

200. What are the ISO 31000 key cost drivers?
<--- Score

201. How is the data gathered?
<--- Score

202. Are you missing ISO 31000 opportunities?
<--- Score

203. How do you see the future of business continuity at the enterprise level?
<--- Score

204. Was a business case (cost/benefit) developed?
<--- Score

205. How do you manage changes in ISO 31000 requirements?
<--- Score

206. Who pays the cost?
<--- Score

207. Who is accountable?
<--- Score

208. Is the work to date meeting requirements?
<--- Score

209. What resources go in to get the desired output?
<--- Score

210. Does the compliance officer review exceptions to your code of ethics?
<--- Score

211. What kind of analytics data will be gathered?
<--- Score

212. Does management culture emphasize the importance of integrity and ethical behavior?
<--- Score

213. What happens to workflows?
<--- Score

214. Can keys be easily copied?
<--- Score

215. Do you have a ISO 31000 success story or case study ready to tell and share?
<--- Score

216. How do you make sense of multiple criteria?
<--- Score

217. If a customer purchases an item today, when are they likely to purchase a complementary item?
<--- Score

218. How do you determine the effectiveness of your strategies?
<--- Score

219. What are the timeframes required to resolve each of the issues/problems?
<--- Score

220. How are consistent ISO 31000 definitions important?
<--- Score

221. Who serves as Compliance Officer?
<--- Score

222. Is any ISO 31000 documentation required?
<--- Score

223. What is the products current release level/ version?
<--- Score

224. Are there any relevant governance or political concerns that could affect how your organization operations?
<--- Score

225. Are all team members qualified for all tasks?
<--- Score

226. Are spreadsheets and software home grown

or purchased from an outside vendor?
<--- Score

227. How will the ISO 31000 data be captured?
<--- Score

228. Does the average call time provided include both inbound and outbound calls?
<--- Score

229. Who is involved with workflow mapping?
<--- Score

230. What output to create?
<--- Score

231. What ISO 31000 standards are applicable?
<--- Score

232. What will it take to meet key stakeholder demands?
<--- Score

233. Do you have any proprietary tools or products related to social media?
<--- Score

234. What are the ISO 31000 business drivers?
<--- Score

235. What is the root cause(s) of the problem?
<--- Score

236. What does a Test Case verify?
<--- Score

237. Which type of crisis and of what order of magnitude is the system designed or targeted to survive?
<--- Score

238. Do you have a mechanism to collect visitor/ customer information?
<--- Score

239. What are the pros and cons of ISO 31000?
<--- Score

240. Does the user have permission to synchronize the address book?
<--- Score

241. Who makes the ISO 31000 decisions in your organization?
<--- Score

242. What size quarterly operating or cash losses has management and the board agreed to tolerable?
<--- Score

243. Which ISO 31000 impacts are significant?
<--- Score

244. At what point will vulnerability assessments be performed once ISO 31000 is put into production (e.g., ongoing Risk Management after implementation)?
<--- Score

245. When should a process be art not science?
<--- Score

246. What creative shifts do you need to take?
<--- Score

247. How do you plan for the cost of succession?
<--- Score

248. Is the user a member of an existing organization?
<--- Score

249. What are your primary costs, revenues, assets?
<--- Score

250. Are corrective actions completed in a timely manner and reported to the board?
<--- Score

251. What is enterprise content management?
<--- Score

252. Has an output goal been set?
<--- Score

253. Is the staff supported by adequate information and communication technology?
<--- Score

254. Who are the ISO 31000 decision makers?
<--- Score

255. What is your decision requirements diagram?
<--- Score

256. Has data output been validated?

<--- Score

257. What type of information may be released?
<--- Score

258. What could happen if you do not do it?
<--- Score

259. How long to keep data and how to manage retention costs?
<--- Score

260. Do you adhere to, or apply, the ISO 31000 Risk Management standard?
<--- Score

261. What volume of mentions has your organization handled in the past (e.g. 2,500 mentions per week)?
<--- Score

262. How to deliver enterprise integrated management information ?
<--- Score

263. Is there an action plan in case of emergencies?
<--- Score

264. What are the costs of delaying ISO 31000 action?
<--- Score

265. Does a good decision guarantee a good outcome?
<--- Score

266. Does the compliance officer have the right level of independence?
<--- Score

267. How do you mitigate ISO 31000 risk?
<--- Score

268. What are the operational costs after ISO 31000 deployment?
<--- Score

269. Are the knowledge and management capabilities available to diversify or add another enterprise?
<--- Score

270. How are ISO 31000 risks managed?
<--- Score

271. What users will be impacted?
<--- Score

272. Are your encryption keys maintained by the cloud consumer or a trusted key management provider?
<--- Score

273. What is the value proposition for senior leadership?
<--- Score

274. How has the ISO 31000 data been gathered?
<--- Score

275. What sort of initial information to gather?

<--- Score

276. How do you structure your account teams?
<--- Score

277. Why every program should be based on ISO 31000 risk management standard?
<--- Score

278. Security settings: what if you can not access a feature?
<--- Score

279. Who needs to know?
<--- Score

280. What languages are supported?
<--- Score

281. Are your recovery strategies regularly updated?
<--- Score

282. Is there effective security over assets including systems, information and vital records?
<--- Score

283. What is the size of loss for a given confidence level?
<--- Score

284. How do you transition from the baseline to the target?
<--- Score

285. How can you reduce the costs of obtaining

inputs?
<--- Score

286. What knowledge or experience is required?
<--- Score

287. How to secure supply chains in an environment where manufacturers barely touch the products they make?
<--- Score

288. Why are you doing ISO 31000 and what is the scope?
<--- Score

289. What drives O&M cost?
<--- Score

290. What is the culture and operating style within and around the business?
<--- Score

291. Can you integrate quality management and risk management?
<--- Score

292. What are the expected ISO 31000 results?
<--- Score

293. How does the accounting information system generate reports?
<--- Score

294. What extra resources will you need?
<--- Score

295. What is the Return on Investment?
<--- Score

296. What qualifications do ISO 31000 leaders need?
<--- Score

297. Are there agreed upon techniques that can be leveraged?
<--- Score

298. Do you have a mechanism in place to quickly respond to visitor/customer inquiries and orders?
<--- Score

299. What happens to customizations?
<--- Score

300. Do you invest in Web self-services?
<--- Score

301. What could cause you to change course?
<--- Score

302. At what cost?
<--- Score

303. Are practices widely used throughout critical infrastructure and industry?
<--- Score

304. What is the output?
<--- Score

305. What qualifications and skills do you need?
<--- Score

306. How many trainings, in total, are needed?
<--- Score

307. What is the oversight process?
<--- Score

308. Are there any revenue recognition issues?
<--- Score

309. What is in scope?
<--- Score

310. Does the compliance officer have all appropriate access and all necessary resources?
<--- Score

311. Are the most efficient solutions problem-specific?
<--- Score

312. Is the cost worth the ISO 31000 effort ?
<--- Score

313. What is the worst case scenario?
<--- Score

314. What is the experience of personnel on this project?
<--- Score

315. Who should make the ISO 31000 decisions?
<--- Score

316. What is out-of-scope initially?
<--- Score

317. Are the key business and technology risks being managed?
<--- Score

318. How do you think BPM companies can contribute to your organizational GRC goals of enterprises?
<--- Score

319. What criteria will you use to assess your ISO 31000 risks?
<--- Score

320. What ISO 31000 data will be collected?
<--- Score

321. Who manages supplier risk management in your organization?
<--- Score

322. Do you know the ISO 31000 risk management standard?
<--- Score

323. What are hidden ISO 31000 quality costs?
<--- Score

324. Do staffs use guidance effectively?
<--- Score

325. Which ISO 31000 solution is appropriate?
<--- Score

326. What do you benefit if certified against ISO 31000?

<--- Score

327. Can visitors/customers register on your website?
<--- Score

328. Will your goals reflect your program budget?
<--- Score

329. How critical is the programs mission or purpose to your organizations mission as a whole?
<--- Score

330. What could happen?
<--- Score

331. How do you verify and develop ideas and innovations?
<--- Score

332. Does a ISO 31000 quantification method exist?
<--- Score

333. What would the effects be if the confidentiality, integrity, and/or availability of the information system were compromised?
<--- Score

334. Is pre-qualification of suppliers carried out?
<--- Score

335. How long should e-mail messages be stored?
<--- Score

336. How do you verify performance?

<--- Score

337. Does the user have permission to synchronize to Outlook?
<--- Score

338. Have you anticipated questions that your visitors or customers might have?
<--- Score

339. What are the ISO 31000 security risks?
<--- Score

340. How do you build resilience into your organizations culture?
<--- Score

341. Does your current records program have the authority to establish an ERM program?
<--- Score

342. Does the compliance officer report directly to the CEO/gc/audit committee?
<--- Score

343. Which ISO 31000 data should be retained?
<--- Score

344. How will ISO 31000 decisions be made and monitored?
<--- Score

345. How difficult is it to qualify what ISO 31000 ROI is?
<--- Score

346. What is a worst-case scenario for losses?
<--- Score

347. Does your organization have a register of compliance obligations?
<--- Score

348. How often does your organization hold a sales activity?
<--- Score

349. Have site safety assessments been undertaken?
<--- Score

350. How is implementation research currently incorporated into each of your goals?
<--- Score

351. Is the ISO 31000 documentation thorough?
<--- Score

352. What are your key vulnerabilities?
<--- Score

353. What question will you ask today that will lead to a better answer tomorrow?
<--- Score

354. When should you bother with diagrams?
<--- Score

355. Do you adhere to best practices interface design?
<--- Score

356. Who is going to spread your message?
<--- Score

357. Are there multiple Outlook profiles?
<--- Score

358. Is your critical infrastructure cyber resistant?
<--- Score

359. How is training accomplished: in person, Web based?
<--- Score

360. Is there a pattern to your clients buying habits (e.g., seasonal)?
<--- Score

361. Is the final output clearly identified?
<--- Score

362. Why a ISO 31000 focus?
<--- Score

363. How are you working with management and stakeholders (especially shareholders) to help the enterprise balance demands for short-term performance and long-term prosperity?
<--- Score

364. How scalable is your ISO 31000 solution?
<--- Score

365. Have the principles under the ERM component internal environment been considered?
<--- Score

366. Do you need to do a usability evaluation?
<--- Score

367. Is there a known outage?
<--- Score

368. What ISO 31000 events should you attend?
<--- Score

369. How is the ISO 31000 Value Stream Mapping managed?
<--- Score

370. Does business continuity and disaster recovery readiness have the support of top management in your organization?
<--- Score

371. What are the performance and scale of the ISO 31000 tools?
<--- Score

372. What do people want to verify?
<--- Score

373. What do you gain from using ISO 31000?
<--- Score

374. What is the Value Stream Mapping?
<--- Score

375. What is your organizations system for selecting qualified vendors?
<--- Score

376. Does management have the right priorities among projects?
<--- Score

377. What are the necessary qualifications?
<--- Score

378. What is the scope of ISO 31000?
<--- Score

379. Is there an assigned professional responsible for the program?
<--- Score

380. What do they buy?
<--- Score

381. Who will be responsible internally?
<--- Score

382. Are decisions made in a timely manner?
<--- Score

383. What are the estimated costs of proposed changes?
<--- Score

384. What can be used to verify compliance?
<--- Score

385. What services do you perform that merit premium margins?
<--- Score

386. Has the volatility of losses been increasing or decreasing over the past five years?

<--- Score

387. Why is this a framework that other organizations should support?
<--- Score

388. Is the quality assurance team identified?
<--- Score

389. Does your customers interact with each other?
<--- Score

390. Why have organizational compliance and erm programs?
<--- Score

391. How does your organization evaluate strategic ISO 31000 success?
<--- Score

392. What assumptions are made about the solution and approach?
<--- Score

393. Do you have a flow diagram of what happens?
<--- Score

394. Is your position full-time or part-time?
<--- Score

395. Is it needed?
<--- Score

396. What would be a real cause for concern?
<--- Score

397. What services can the internal auditors provide for the audit committee?
<--- Score

398. When do they buy?
<--- Score

399. Is there a reporting system that allows anonymous reporting, protecting identities to the extent permitted by law and consistent with the policies of your organizations Code of Conduct?
<--- Score

400. Did you miss any major ISO 31000 issues?
<--- Score

401. How to integrate different management systems?
<--- Score

402. How widespread is its use?
<--- Score

403. What are the internal constraints which limit freedom of action or choice?
<--- Score

404. What systems/processes must you excel at?
<--- Score

405. What are the ISO 31000 investment costs?
<--- Score

406. What is your organizations history of meeting recovery time objectives?

<--- Score

407. Does hedging affect organization value?
<--- Score

408. Do you have the authority to produce the output?
<--- Score

409. How do you benefit from the ISO 31000 certification?
<--- Score

410. Who approved the ISO 31000 scope?
<--- Score

411. What is the scope of the ISO 31000 work?
<--- Score

412. What and how many inventories should be stocked at each stage of a supply chain?
<--- Score

413. Do vendor agreements bring new compliance risk ?
<--- Score

414. Who should resolve the ISO 31000 issues?
<--- Score

415. How do you build the right business case?
<--- Score

416. Do you have an issue in getting priority?
<--- Score

417. How does your organization know that its ERM is succeeding?
<--- Score

418. How do you gather the stories?
<--- Score

419. What are evaluation criteria for the output?
<--- Score

420. Which needs are not included or involved?
<--- Score

421. What is the ISO 31000 business impact?
<--- Score

422. Do regular business reports include compliance matters?
<--- Score

423. How do customers communicate with you?
<--- Score

424. What does your operating model cost?
<--- Score

425. Are the management and other pivotal/ critical roles staffed by competent people?
<--- Score

426. Is the staff appropriate for the work?
<--- Score

427. Do staff qualifications match your project?
<--- Score

428. What are the requirements for audit information?
<--- Score

429. What training and qualifications will you need?
<--- Score

430. Is there a major disconnect in terms of quality and efficiency between different content and records management functions in the enterprise?
<--- Score

431. Are the ISO 31000 requirements testable?
<--- Score

432. Are enterprise and IT objectives linked and synchronized?
<--- Score

433. What is the vendors reach in a particular market?
<--- Score

434. Do you have organizational privacy requirements?
<--- Score

435. How do you verify the authenticity of the data and information used?
<--- Score

436. Are all staff in core ISO 31000 subjects Highly Qualified?
<--- Score

437. What does compliance do with the information?
<--- Score

438. Is the required ISO 31000 data gathered?
<--- Score

439. How will the data be checked for quality?
<--- Score

440. Does the scope remain the same?
<--- Score

441. Do you follow-up with your customers after order has been filled?
<--- Score

442. How many times do other organizations ask new organization graduates to apply education?
<--- Score

443. How does management assess whether all components operate together ?
<--- Score

444. Is the scope of ISO 31000 cost analysis cost-effective?
<--- Score

445. How do you monitor usage and cost?
<--- Score

446. Are actual costs in line with budgeted costs?
<--- Score

447. What is your plan to assess your security

risks?
<--- Score

448. How do you spread information?
<--- Score

449. Can customers place orders online?
<--- Score

450. What are the roles and responsibilities of business unit and divisional management?
<--- Score

451. Do you have the optimal project management team structure?
<--- Score

452. What is the involvement of executive staff , middle management, and staff ?
<--- Score

453. Is the ISO 31000 test/monitoring cost justified?
<--- Score

454. What is the ISO 31000 Driver?
<--- Score

455. What is your core business and how will it evolve in the future?
<--- Score

456. What protections do you want from your organizations D&O insurance policy?
<--- Score

457. What risks do you need to manage?
<--- Score

458. Is this intended for private organizations?
<--- Score

459. Is your organization achieving optimum use of its resources?
<--- Score

460. What do you need to qualify?
<--- Score

461. How do you tailor your reports for the board and executive management?
<--- Score

462. What type of information may be released to whom?
<--- Score

463. How should the various cloud services integrate with the existing enterprise security architecture?
<--- Score

464. Who is in charge of ensuring that the repair is made?
<--- Score

465. Does the user have permission to create activities?
<--- Score

466. What laws and regulations apply to your organization?

<--- Score

467. What should be the private sectors involvement in the future governance of the Framework?
<--- Score

468. How engaged is senior management?
<--- Score

469. What promises have been made?
<--- Score

470. Who needs budgets?
<--- Score

471. What happens if cost savings do not materialize?
<--- Score

472. Is there a clear ISO 31000 case definition?
<--- Score

473. What is the scope of the ISO 31000 effort?
<--- Score

474. Are your outputs consistent?
<--- Score

475. Does your organization dismiss/discipline high level managers for violations?
<--- Score

476. What has been the most positive outcome of this information exchange?
<--- Score

477. Who owns what data?
<--- Score

478. What are the ISO 31000 resources needed?
<--- Score

479. What ISO 31000 data should be collected?
<--- Score

480. Where do you need to exercise leadership?
<--- Score

481. Is expert judgment used in the model or method?
<--- Score

482. Where do the ISO 31000 decisions reside?
<--- Score

483. Who is involved in the management review process?
<--- Score

484. Do you keep key information backed up, maintained, and tested periodically?
<--- Score

485. Do the people involved in content and records management have the right skills to achieve your strategic and tactical goals?
<--- Score

486. What is out of scope?
<--- Score

487. What is the complexity of the output produced?
<--- Score

488. How can the phases of ISO 31000 development be identified?
<--- Score

489. What are the core elements of the ISO 31000 business case?
<--- Score

490. What will reporting to executive management and the Board look like going forward?
<--- Score

491. What is the overall talent health of your organization as a whole at senior levels, and for each organization reporting to a member of the Senior Leadership Team?
<--- Score

492. Are the ISO 31000 standards challenging?
<--- Score

493. What is the problem and/or vulnerability?
<--- Score

494. What are your organizations future claims or liabilities likely to be?
<--- Score

Add up total points for this section:
_____ = Total points for this section

Divided by: ______ (number of

statements answered) = ______
Average score for this section

Transfer your score to the ISO 31000 Index at the beginning of the Self-Assessment.

ISO 31000 and Managing Projects, Criteria for Project Managers:

1.0 Initiating Process Group: ISO 31000

1. Establishment of pm office?

2. Does the ISO 31000 project team have enough people to execute the ISO 31000 project plan?

3. Were decisions made in a timely manner?

4. The ISO 31000 project you are managing has nine stakeholders. How many channel of communications are there between corresponding stakeholders?

5. What is the NEXT thing to do?

6. The ISO 31000 project managers have maximum authority in which type of organization?

7. What will be the pressing issues of tomorrow?

8. What are the tools and techniques to be used in each phase?

9. Which of six sigmas dmaic phases focuses on the measurement of internal process that affect factors that are critical to quality?

10. How well did you do?

11. What are the short and long term implications?

12. How well did the chosen processes produce the expected results?

13. Are you properly tracking the progress of the ISO 31000 project and communicating the status to stakeholders?

14. Have you evaluated the teams performance and asked for feedback?

15. Were escalated issues resolved promptly?

16. What will you do?

17. Who is behind the ISO 31000 project?

18. What communication items need improvement?

19. Where must it be done?

1.1 Project Charter: ISO 31000

20. Who will take notes, document decisions?

21. Are there special technology requirements?

22. What goes into your ISO 31000 project Charter?

23. How are ISO 31000 projects different from operations?

24. Are you building in-house ?

25. Why the improvements?

26. Who is the ISO 31000 project Manager?

27. What are the known stakeholder requirements?

28. Why is a ISO 31000 project Charter used?

29. Why Outsource?

30. ISO 31000 project deliverables: what is the ISO 31000 project going to produce?

31. What barriers do you predict to your success?

32. Where and how does the team fit within your organization structure?

33. How will you learn more about the process or system you are trying to improve?

34. What are the constraints?

35. Pop quiz – which are the same inputs as in the ISO 31000 project charter?

36. Who manages integration?

37. Name and describe the elements that deal with providing the detail?

38. Why executive support?

39. Did your ISO 31000 project ask for this?

1.2 Stakeholder Register: ISO 31000

40. What & Why?

41. Who is managing stakeholder engagement?

42. Who are the stakeholders?

43. What opportunities exist to provide communications?

44. Who wants to talk about Security?

45. What are the major ISO 31000 project milestones requiring communications or providing communications opportunities?

46. How should employers make voices heard?

47. How much influence do they have on the ISO 31000 project?

48. Is your organization ready for change?

49. What is the power of the stakeholder?

50. How will reports be created?

51. How big is the gap?

1.3 Stakeholder Analysis Matrix: ISO 31000

52. New USPs?

53. Competitor intentions - various?

54. What are the reimbursement requirements?

55. Technology development and innovation?

56. Vital contracts and partners?

57. Are you working on the right risks?

58. If the baseline is now, and if its improved it will be better than now?

59. Loss of key staff?

60. Continuity, supply chain robustness?

61. What actions can be taken to reduce or mitigate risk?

62. How do rules, behaviors affect stakes?

63. How to involve media?

64. Resource providers; who can provide resources to ensure the implementation of the ISO 31000 project?

65. What can the stakeholder prevent from

happening?

66. Which conditions out of the control of the management are crucial for the sustainability of its effects?

67. What are innovative aspects of your organization?

68. Is there evidence that demonstrates the impact of education on the ISO 31000 projects outcomes?

69. Political effects?

70. It developments?

71. How are you predicting what future (work)loads will be?

2.0 Planning Process Group: ISO 31000

72. When developing the estimates for ISO 31000 project phases, you choose to add the individual estimates for the activities that comprise each phase. What type of estimation method are you using?

73. Are there efficient coordination mechanisms to avoid overloading the counterparts, participating stakeholders?

74. How well did the chosen processes fit the needs of the ISO 31000 project?

75. Are you just doing busywork to pass the time?

76. Does it make any difference if you are successful?

77. On which process should team members spend the most time?

78. How well defined and documented are the ISO 31000 project management processes you chose to use?

79. What input will you be required to provide the ISO 31000 project team?

80. How can you tell when you are done?

81. Does the program have follow-up mechanisms (to verify the quality of the products, punctuality of

delivery, etc.) to measure progress in the achievement of the envisaged results?

82. What should you do next?

83. You did your readings, yes?

84. How does activity resource estimation affect activity duration estimation?

85. Is the pace of implementing the products of the program ensuring the completeness of the results of the ISO 31000 project?

86. How will users learn how to use the deliverables?

87. What is the difference between the early schedule and late schedule?

88. In what way has the program contributed towards the issue culture and development included on the public agenda?

89. What types of differentiated effects are resulting from the ISO 31000 project and to what extent?

90. If action is called for, what form should it take?

91. How will you do it?

2.1 Project Management Plan: ISO 31000

92. Is the appropriate plan selected based on your organizations objectives and evaluation criteria expressed in Principles and Guidelines policies?

93. Are there any scope changes proposed for a previously authorized ISO 31000 project?

94. Is mitigation authorized or recommended?

95. Is there an incremental analysis/cost effectiveness analysis of proposed mitigation features based on an approved method and using an accepted model?

96. What are the assumptions?

97. What does management expect of PMs?

98. Does the selected plan protect privacy?

99. If the ISO 31000 project is complex or scope is specialized, do you have appropriate and/or qualified staff available to perform the tasks?

100. Are the proposed ISO 31000 project purposes different than a previously authorized ISO 31000 project?

101. Development trends and opportunities. What if the positive direction and vision of your organization causes expected trends to change?

102. Are calculations and results of analyzes essentially correct?

103. Are cost risk analysis methods applied to develop contingencies for the estimated total ISO 31000 project costs?

104. What would you do differently?

105. Are the existing and future without-plan conditions reasonable and appropriate?

106. Is there anything you would now do differently on your ISO 31000 project based on past experience?

107. Who is the ISO 31000 project Manager?

108. What is ISO 31000 project scope management?

109. Is the engineering content at a feasibility level-of-detail, and is it sufficiently complete, to provide an adequate basis for the baseline cost estimate?

110. Why Change?

2.2 Scope Management Plan: ISO 31000

111. Given the scope of the ISO 31000 project, which criterion should be optimized?

112. What do you need to do to accomplish the goal or goals?

113. Are there checklists created to demine if all quality processes are followed?

114. Are corrective actions and variances reported?

115. Is there an on-going process in place to monitor ISO 31000 project risks?

116. Cost / benefit analysis?

117. What weaknesses do you have?

118. Are measurements and feedback mechanisms incorporated in tracking work effort & refining work estimating techniques?

119. Have the procedures for identifying budget variances been followed?

120. Have adequate procedures been put in place for ISO 31000 project communication and status reporting across ISO 31000 project boundaries (for example interdependent software development among interfacing systems)?

121. Are decisions captured in a decisions log?

122. Are milestone deliverables effectively tracked and compared to ISO 31000 project plan?

123. Are all key components of a Quality Assurance Plan present?

124. Are you doing what you have set out to do?

125. When is corrective or preventative action required?

126. Where do scope processes fit in?

127. How much money have you spent?

128. Are risk triggers captured?

129. What work performance data will be captured?

130. Are issues raised, assessed, actioned, and resolved in a timely and efficient manner?

2.3 Requirements Management Plan: ISO 31000

131. What went wrong?

132. Who will approve the requirements (and if multiple approvers, in what order)?

133. Have stakeholders been instructed in the Change Control process?

134. Who will finally present the work or product(s) for acceptance?

135. Is any organizational data being used or stored?

136. What performance metrics will be used?

137. What is a problem?

138. Will the contractors involved take full responsibility?

139. Who will do the reporting and to whom will reports be delivered?

140. Is it new or replacing an existing business system or process?

141. Is the system software (non-operating system) new to the IT ISO 31000 project team?

142. Will you use an assessment of the ISO 31000

project environment as a tool to discover risk to the requirements process?

143. Are actual resource expenditures versus planned still acceptable?

144. Did you avoid subjective, flowery or non-specific statements?

145. Is there formal agreement on who has authority to request a change in requirements?

146. Controlling ISO 31000 project requirements involves monitoring the status of the ISO 31000 project requirements and managing changes to the requirements. Who is responsible for monitoring and tracking the ISO 31000 project requirements?

147. Subject to change control?

148. What information regarding the ISO 31000 project requirements will be reported?

149. How knowledgeable is the primary Stakeholder(s) in the proposed application area?

150. What are you trying to do?

2.4 Requirements Documentation: ISO 31000

151. How do you know when a Requirement is accurate enough?

152. How do you get the user to tell you what they want?

153. Is your business case still valid?

154. Completeness. are all functions required by the customer included?

155. What is effective documentation?

156. How does what is being described meet the business need?

157. How to document system requirements?

158. How does the proposed ISO 31000 project contribute to the overall objectives of your organization?

159. How will requirements be documented and who signs off on them?

160. What are current process problems?

161. Where are business rules being captured?

162. Consistency. are there any requirements

conflicts?

163. Where do you define what is a customer, what are the attributes of customer?

164. How will they be documented / shared?

165. Is the origin of the requirement clearly stated?

166. Who is interacting with the system?

167. What facilities must be supported by the system?

168. What images does it conjure?

169. How can you document system requirements?

2.5 Requirements Traceability Matrix: ISO 31000

170. How do you manage scope?

171. Describe the process for approving requirements so they can be added to the traceability matrix and ISO 31000 project work can be performed. Will the ISO 31000 project requirements become approved in writing?

172. Why use a WBS?

173. What is the WBS?

174. Will you use a Requirements Traceability Matrix?

175. How small is small enough?

176. What percentage of ISO 31000 projects are producing traceability matrices between requirements and other work products?

177. How will it affect the stakeholders personally in career?

178. Is there a requirements traceability process in place?

179. Why do you manage scope?

180. What are the chronologies, contingencies, consequences, criteria?

181. Do you have a clear understanding of all subcontracts in place?

2.6 Project Scope Statement: ISO 31000

182. Are there issues that could affect the existing requirements for the result, service, or product if the scope changes?

183. Are there adequate ISO 31000 project control systems?

184. Was planning completed before the ISO 31000 project was initiated?

185. Will you need a statement of work?

186. What should you drop in order to add something new?

187. Elements of scope management that deal with concept development ?

188. Is the change control process documented and on file?

189. Is the quality function identified and assigned?

190. How often will scope changes be reviewed?

191. Will statistics related to QA be collected, trends analyzed, and problems raised as issues?

192. Has the ISO 31000 project scope statement been reviewed as part of the baseline process?

193. Is there a baseline plan against which to measure progress?

194. Change management vs. change leadership - what is the difference?

195. Are the input requirements from the team members clearly documented and communicated?

196. Risks?

197. Is the ISO 31000 project manager qualified and experienced in ISO 31000 project management?

198. Elements that deal with providing the detail?

199. Are there completion/verification criteria defined for each task producing an output?

2.7 Assumption and Constraint Log: ISO 31000

200. What do you audit?

201. Are best practices and metrics employed to identify issues, progress, performance, etc.?

202. Would known impacts serve as impediments?

203. Have all necessary approvals been obtained?

204. Are funding and staffing resource estimates sufficiently detailed and documented for use in planning and tracking the ISO 31000 project?

205. Do documented requirements exist for all critical components and areas, including technical, business, interfaces, performance, security and conversion requirements?

206. Is the amount of effort justified by the anticipated value of forming a new process?

207. If appropriate, is the deliverable content consistent with current ISO 31000 project documents and in compliance with the Document Management Plan?

208. What threats might prevent you from getting there?

209. Have all stakeholders been identified?

210. Do you know what your customers expectations are regarding this process?

211. Does the traceability documentation describe the tool and/or mechanism to be used to capture traceability throughout the life cycle?

212. Should factors be unpredictable over time?

213. How many ISO 31000 project staff does this specific process affect?

214. Does the system design reflect the requirements?

215. Are there cosmetic errors that hinder readability and comprehension?

216. Have all involved stakeholders and work groups committed to the ISO 31000 project?

217. Is the steering committee active in ISO 31000 project oversight?

218. Is the definition of the ISO 31000 project scope clear; what needs to be accomplished?

2.8 Work Breakdown Structure: ISO 31000

219. How much detail?

220. Is it still viable?

221. Is it a change in scope?

222. Why would you develop a Work Breakdown Structure?

223. When would you develop a Work Breakdown Structure?

224. Can you make it?

225. When does it have to be done?

226. What is the probability of completing the ISO 31000 project in less that xx days?

227. When do you stop?

228. How many levels?

229. Is the work breakdown structure (wbs) defined and is the scope of the ISO 31000 project clear with assigned deliverable owners?

230. Do you need another level?

231. What is the probability that the ISO 31000 project

duration will exceed xx weeks?

232. How far down?

233. Where does it take place?

234. How big is a work-package?

235. Who has to do it?

2.9 WBS Dictionary: ISO 31000

236. All cwbs elements specified for external reporting?

237. Are retroactive changes to budgets for completed work specifically prohibited in an established procedure, and is this procedure adhered to?

238. Are direct or indirect cost adjustments being accomplished according to accounting procedures acceptable to us?

239. The total budget for the contract (including estimates for authorized and unpriced work)?

240. Are control accounts opened and closed based on the start and completion of work contained therein?

241. Do the lines of authority for incurring indirect costs correspond to the lines of responsibility for management control of the same components of costs?

242. Is future work which cannot be planned in detail subdivided to the extent practicable for budgeting and scheduling purposes?

243. What went right?

244. What size should a work package be?

245. Are data elements reconcilable between internal summary reports and reports forwarded to us?

246. Does the accounting system provide a basis for auditing records of direct costs chargeable to the contract?

247. Does the contractors system provide for accurate cost accumulation and assignment to control accounts in a manner consistent with the budgets using recognized acceptable costing techniques?

248. Should you include sub-activities?

249. Software specification, development, integration, and testing, licenses ?

250. Budgets assigned to control accounts?

251. The ISO 31000 projected business base for each period?

252. Performance to date and material commitment?

253. Cwbs elements to be subcontracted, with identification of subcontractors?

254. Are work packages assigned to performing organizations?

255. Does the scheduling system provide for the identification of work progress against technical and other milestones, and also provide for forecasts of completion dates of scheduled work?

2.10 Schedule Management Plan: ISO 31000

256. Were the budget estimates reasonable?

257. Are target dates established for each milestone deliverable?

258. Is the schedule updated on a periodic basis?

259. Are ISO 31000 project team members committed fulltime?

260. How do you manage time?

261. Does the ISO 31000 project have a formal ISO 31000 project Charter?

262. Are there checklists created to determine if all quality processes are followed?

263. Are ISO 31000 project team members involved in detailed estimating and scheduling?

264. Can be realistically shortened (the duration of subsequent tasks)?

265. Has a provision been made to reassess ISO 31000 project risks at various ISO 31000 project stages?

266. Is it standard practice to formally commit stakeholders to the ISO 31000 project via agreements?

267. Does all ISO 31000 project documentation reside in a common repository for easy access?

268. Has a capability assessment been conducted?

269. Are post milestone ISO 31000 project reviews (PMPR) conducted with your organization at least once a year?

270. ISO 31000 project definition & scope?

271. Are there any activities or deliverables being added or gold-plated that could be dropped or scaled back without falling short of the original requirement?

272. Why conduct schedule analysis?

273. Is the correct WBS element identified for each task and milestone in the IMS?

274. Has the ISO 31000 project scope been baselined?

275. What does a valid Schedule look like?

2.11 Activity List: ISO 31000

276. How should ongoing costs be monitored to try to keep the ISO 31000 project within budget?

277. What went well?

278. What did not go as well?

279. Can you determine the activity that must finish, before this activity can start?

280. What will be performed?

281. How much slack is available in the ISO 31000 project?

282. What are the critical bottleneck activities?

283. What are you counting on?

284. Is infrastructure setup part of your ISO 31000 project?

285. In what sequence?

286. How will it be performed?

287. What is the total time required to complete the ISO 31000 project if no delays occur?

288. What is your organizations history in doing similar activities?

289. Is there anything planned that does not need to be here?

290. What is the LF and LS for each activity?

291. Where will it be performed?

292. Who will perform the work?

293. How do you determine the late start (LS) for each activity?

2.12 Activity Attributes: ISO 31000

294. Time for overtime?

295. Activity: fair or not fair?

296. How difficult will it be to do specific activities on this ISO 31000 project?

297. What conclusions/generalizations can you draw from this?

298. Where else does it apply?

299. What is missing?

300. Have constraints been applied to the start and finish milestones for the phases?

301. Can you re-assign any activities to another resource to resolve an over-allocation?

302. Why?

303. Have you identified the Activity Leveling Priority code value on each activity?

304. What activity do you think you should spend the most time on?

305. Does your organization of the data change its meaning?

306. Would you consider either of corresponding

activities an outlier?

307. Which method produces the more accurate cost assignment?

308. Is there a trend during the year?

309. What is the general pattern here?

310. Were there other ways you could have organized the data to achieve similar results?

311. Can more resources be added?

312. Activity: what is Missing?

313. How many days do you need to complete the work scope with a limit of X number of resources?

2.13 Milestone List: ISO 31000

314. When will the ISO 31000 project be complete?

315. Environmental effects?

316. Insurmountable weaknesses?

317. Information and research?

318. Milestone pages should display the UserID of the person who added the milestone. Does a report or query exist that provides this audit information?

319. What has been done so far?

320. What background experience, skills, and strengths does the team bring to your organization?

321. Level of the Innovation?

322. How soon can the activity finish?

323. Marketing - reach, distribution, awareness?

324. Timescales, deadlines and pressures?

325. Do you foresee any technical risks or developmental challenges?

326. Global influences?

327. What would happen if a delivery of material was one week late?

328. Describe the concept of the technology, product or service that will be or has been developed. How will it be used?

329. Who will manage the ISO 31000 project on a day-to-day basis?

330. It is to be a narrative text providing the crucial aspects of your ISO 31000 project proposal answering what, who, how, when and where?

331. Sustaining internal capabilities?

332. What specific improvements did you make to the ISO 31000 project proposal since the previous time?

333. Effects on core activities, distraction?

2.14 Network Diagram: ISO 31000

334. Where do you schedule uncertainty time?

335. If x is long, what would be the completion time if you break x into two parallel parts of y weeks and z weeks?

336. What activities must follow this activity?

337. What is the lowest cost to complete this ISO 31000 project in xx weeks?

338. What job or jobs follow it?

339. What are the Key Success Factors?

340. Exercise: what is the probability that the ISO 31000 project duration will exceed xx weeks?

341. What activity must be completed immediately before this activity can start?

342. Review the logical flow of the network diagram. Take a look at which activities you have first and then sequence the activities. Do they make sense?

343. What to do and When?

344. What must be completed before an activity can be started?

345. What activities must occur simultaneously with this activity?

346. Where do schedules come from?

347. What controls the start and finish of a job?

348. How confident can you be in your milestone dates and the delivery date?

349. Will crashing x weeks return more in benefits than it costs?

350. What are the Major Administrative Issues?

351. What job or jobs could run concurrently?

352. If the ISO 31000 project network diagram cannot change and you have extra personnel resources, what is the BEST thing to do?

2.15 Activity Resource Requirements: ISO 31000

353. Which logical relationship does the PDM use most often?

354. Are there unresolved issues that need to be addressed?

355. What is the Work Plan Standard?

356. Anything else?

357. When does monitoring begin?

358. Other support in specific areas?

359. Organizational Applicability?

360. Do you use tools like decomposition and rolling-wave planning to produce the activity list and other outputs?

361. How many signatures do you require on a check and does this match what is in your policy and procedures?

362. Why do you do that?

363. What are constraints that you might find during the Human Resource Planning process?

364. How do you handle petty cash?

2.16 Resource Breakdown Structure: ISO 31000

365. Goals for the ISO 31000 project. What is each stakeholders desired outcome for the ISO 31000 project?

366. Who needs what information?

367. What is the difference between % Complete and % work?

368. Changes based on input from stakeholders?

369. What is the purpose of assigning and documenting responsibility?

370. Any changes from stakeholders?

371. Why do you do it?

372. What is each stakeholders desired outcome for the ISO 31000 project?

373. Why time management?

374. Which resource planning tool provides information on resource responsibility and accountability?

375. What is the primary purpose of the human resource plan?

376. Why is this important?

377. Who is allowed to see what data about which resources?

378. How should the information be delivered?

379. Who will be used as a ISO 31000 project team member?

2.17 Activity Duration Estimates: ISO 31000

380. (Cpi), and schedule performance index (spi) for the ISO 31000 project?

381. Do procedures exist describing how the ISO 31000 project scope will be managed?

382. Are costs that may be needed to account for ISO 31000 project risks determined?

383. Are risks that are likely to affect the ISO 31000 project identified and documented?

384. Are procedures followed to ensure information is available to stakeholders in a timely manner?

385. When would a milestone chart be used instead of a bar char?

386. Are processes defined to monitor ISO 31000 project cost and schedule variances?

387. What is the BEST thing for the ISO 31000 project manager to do?

388. What is involved in the solicitation process?

389. Why is there a growing trend in outsourcing, especially in the government?

390. How can others help ISO 31000 project managers

understand your organizational context for ISO 31000 projects?

391. Are team building activities completed to improve team performance?

392. Why is outsourcing growing so rapidly?

393. Will additional funds be needed for hardware or software?

394. What type of people would you want on your team?

395. What are the main types of contracts if you do decide to outsource?

396. After how many days will the lease cost be the same as the purchase cost for the equipment?

397. What do you think the real problem was in this case?

398. Which is the BEST ISO 31000 project management tool to use to determine the longest time the ISO 31000 project will take?

399. What is pmp certification, and why do you think the number of people earning it has grown so much in the past ten years?

2.18 Duration Estimating Worksheet: ISO 31000

400. Can the ISO 31000 project be constructed as planned?

401. What utility impacts are there?

402. What is your role?

403. What questions do you have?

404. For other activities, how much delay can be tolerated?

405. How can the ISO 31000 project be displayed graphically to better visualize the activities?

406. How should ongoing costs be monitored to try to keep the ISO 31000 project within budget?

407. What work will be included in the ISO 31000 project?

408. What info is needed?

409. Why estimate time and cost?

410. What is cost and ISO 31000 project cost management?

411. Will the ISO 31000 project collaborate with the local community and leverage resources?

412. Define the work as completely as possible. What work will be included in the ISO 31000 project?

413. Value pocket identification & quantification what are value pockets?

414. Is this operation cost effective?

415. Is the ISO 31000 project responsive to community need?

416. Small or large ISO 31000 project?

2.19 Project Schedule: ISO 31000

417. Have all ISO 31000 project delays been adequately accounted for, communicated to all stakeholders and adjustments made in overall ISO 31000 project schedule?

418. If you can not fix it, how do you do it differently?

419. Are all remaining durations correct?

420. What documents, if any, will the subcontractor provide (eg ISO 31000 project schedule, quality plan etc)?

421. Did the ISO 31000 project come in under budget?

422. How closely did the initial ISO 31000 project Schedule compare with the actual schedule?

423. If there are any qualifying green components to this ISO 31000 project, what portion of the total ISO 31000 project cost is green?

424. Why do you need schedules?

425. Is the ISO 31000 project schedule available for all ISO 31000 project team members to review?

426. Why do you need to manage ISO 31000 project Risk?

427. Is ISO 31000 project work proceeding in

accordance with the original ISO 31000 project schedule?

428. How detailed should a ISO 31000 project get?

429. Why is software ISO 31000 project disaster so common?

430. Did the ISO 31000 project come in on schedule?

431. ISO 31000 project work estimates Who is managing the work estimate quality of work tasks in the ISO 31000 project schedule?

432. What is ISO 31000 project management?

433. Schedule/cost recovery?

434. How do you use schedules?

2.20 Cost Management Plan: ISO 31000

435. Are metrics used to evaluate and manage Vendors?

436. Is the steering committee active in ISO 31000 project oversight?

437. Do ISO 31000 project teams & team members report on status / activities / progress?

438. Pareto diagrams, statistical sampling, flow charting or trend analysis used quality monitoring?

439. Has a provision been made to reassess ISO 31000 project risks at various ISO 31000 project stages?

440. What is your organizations history in doing similar tasks?

441. Is there a requirements change management processes in place?

442. Are procurement deliverables arriving on time and to specification?

443. Similar ISO 31000 projects?

444. Is your organization certified as a supplier, wholesaler and/or regular dealer?

445. Is documentation created for communication

with the suppliers and Vendors?

446. Are staff skills known and available for each task?

447. Is stakeholder involvement adequate?

448. Is there a formal set of procedures supporting Stakeholder Management?

449. If you sold 10x widgets on a day, what would the affect on costs be?

450. Have adequate resources been provided by management to ensure ISO 31000 project success?

451. Weve met your goals?

452. What strengths do you have?

453. Is quality monitored from the perspective of the customers needs and expectations?

2.21 Activity Cost Estimates: ISO 31000

454. How Award?

455. Does the estimator estimate by task or by person?

456. Padding is bad and contingencies are good. what is the difference?

457. Maintenance Reserve?

458. How do you allocate indirect costs to activities?

459. How do you treat administrative costs in the activity inventory?

460. Can you delete activities or make them inactive?

461. How do you change activities?

462. Specific - is the objective clear in terms of what, how, when, and where the situation will be changed?

463. What makes a good activity description?

464. What were things that you did very well and want to do the same again on the next ISO 31000 project?

465. What makes a good expected result statement?

466. How do you fund change orders?

467. Did the ISO 31000 project team have the right skills?

468. What is the activity inventory?

469. Where can you get activity reports?

470. How many activities should you have?

471. Will you need to provide essential services information about activities?

472. Which contract type places the most risk on the seller?

2.22 Cost Estimating Worksheet: ISO 31000

473. What can be included?

474. What costs are to be estimated?

475. Is it feasible to establish a control group arrangement?

476. What is the estimated labor cost today based upon this information?

477. How will the results be shared and to whom?

478. Who is best positioned to know and assist in identifying corresponding factors?

479. What additional ISO 31000 project(s) could be initiated as a result of this ISO 31000 project?

480. Will the ISO 31000 project collaborate with the local community and leverage resources?

481. Does the ISO 31000 project provide innovative ways for stakeholders to overcome obstacles or deliver better outcomes?

482. Identify the timeframe necessary to monitor progress and collect data to determine how the selected measure has changed?

483. What is the purpose of estimating?

484. What will others want?

485. Ask: are others positioned to know, are others credible, and will others cooperate?

486. What happens to any remaining funds not used?

487. Can a trend be established from historical performance data on the selected measure and are the criteria for using trend analysis or forecasting methods met?

488. Is the ISO 31000 project responsive to community need?

2.23 Cost Baseline: ISO 31000

489. On budget?

490. Are you asking management for something as a result of this update?

491. Have the resources used by the ISO 31000 project been reassigned to other units or ISO 31000 projects?

492. What is the most important thing to do next to make your ISO 31000 project successful?

493. Should a more thorough impact analysis be conducted?

494. How likely is it to go wrong?

495. Are there contingencies or conditions related to the acceptance?

496. Have all the product or service deliverables been accepted by the customer?

497. Are procedures defined by which the cost baseline may be changed?

498. Have the actual milestone completion dates been compared to the approved schedule?

499. Eac -estimate at completion, what is the total job expected to cost?

500. Does a process exist for establishing a cost

baseline to measure ISO 31000 project performance?

501. Is request in line with priorities?

502. What is cost and ISO 31000 project cost management?

503. Have the lessons learned been filed with the ISO 31000 project Management Office?

504. Does the suggested change request seem to represent a necessary enhancement to the product?

505. How long are you willing to wait before you find out were late?

506. What can go wrong?

507. What is it ?

508. Does the suggested change request represent a desired enhancement to the products functionality?

2.24 Quality Management Plan: ISO 31000

509. Who is responsible?

510. Sampling part of task?

511. What are you trying to accomplish?

512. What would you gain if you spent time working to improve this process?

513. What methods are used?

514. Is a component/condition present?

515. Is there a Quality Management Plan?

516. Are there processes in place to ensure internal consistency between the source code components?

517. What is the Difference Between a QMP and QAPP?

518. How are new requirements or changes to requirements identified?

519. When reporting to different audiences, do you vary the form or type of report?

520. How is staff trained in procedures?

521. How do you document and correct

nonconformances?

522. How do you decide who is responsible for signing the data reports?

523. How do senior leaders create and communicate values and performance expectations?

524. Does a documented ISO 31000 project organizational policy & plan (i.e. governance model) exist?

525. Meet how often?

526. Does a prospective decision remain the same regardless of what the data show is?

2.25 Quality Metrics: ISO 31000

527. What does this tell us?

528. Where is quality now?

529. What metrics do you measure?

530. Which are the right metrics to use?

531. Are applicable standards referenced and available?

532. What documentation is required?

533. Are quality metrics defined?

534. What do you measure?

535. What is the benchmark?

536. What percentage are outcome-based?

537. Is there alignment within your organization on definitions?

538. What makes a visualization memorable?

539. What level of statistical confidence do you use?

540. Has risk analysis been adequately reviewed?

541. Product Availability ?

542. How do you calculate such metrics?

543. What happens if you get an abnormal result?

544. Is a risk containment plan in place?

545. Which data do others need in one place to target areas of improvement?

2.26 Process Improvement Plan: ISO 31000

546. What is the return on investment?

547. Who should prepare the process improvement action plan?

548. Where do you focus?

549. Modeling current processes is great, and will you ever see a return on that investment?

550. Have the supporting tools been developed or acquired?

551. What lessons have you learned so far?

552. What personnel are the sponsors for that initiative?

553. Are you making progress on the goals?

554. Does your process ensure quality?

555. Does explicit definition of the measures exist?

556. Are you meeting the quality standards?

557. What personnel are the change agents for your initiative?

558. What actions are needed to address the

problems and achieve the goals?

559. Why do you want to achieve the goal?

560. The motive is determined by asking, Why do you want to achieve this goal?

561. Have the frequency of collection and the points in the process where measurements will be made been determined?

562. Has the time line required to move measurement results from the points of collection to databases or users been established?

563. How do you manage quality?

564. What personnel are the champions for the initiative?

2.27 Responsibility Assignment Matrix: ISO 31000

565. Budgets assigned to major functional organizations?

566. Is the anticipated (firm and potential) business base ISO 31000 projected in a rational, consistent manner?

567. Not any rs, as, or cs: if an identified role is only informed, should others be eliminated from the matrix?

568. What travel needed?

569. Incurrence of actual indirect costs in excess of budgets, by element of expense?

570. Is data disseminated to the contractors management timely, accurate, and usable?

571. Is work progressively subdivided into detailed work packages as requirements are defined?

572. Changes in the nature of the overhead requirements?

573. Contemplated overhead expenditure for each period based on the best information currently available?

574. Are indirect costs charged to the appropriate

indirect pools and incurring organization?

575. Detailed schedules which support control account and work package start and completion dates/events?

576. Are significant decision points, constraints, and interfaces identified as key milestones?

577. How do you manage remotely to staff in other Divisions?

578. Are detailed work packages planned as far in advance as practicable?

579. No rs: if a task has no one listed as responsible, who is getting the job done?

580. The staff interests – is the group or the person interested in working for this ISO 31000 project?

581. What simple tool can you use to help identify and prioritize ISO 31000 project risks that is very low tech and high touch?

582. What expertise is available in your department?

583. Budgeted cost for work performed?

2.28 Roles and Responsibilities: ISO 31000

584. Is there a training program in place for stakeholders covering expectations, roles and responsibilities and any addition knowledge others need to be good stakeholders?

585. What specific behaviors did you observe?

586. Who: who is involved?

587. What are your major roles and responsibilities in the area of performance measurement and assessment?

588. How well did the ISO 31000 project Team understand the expectations of specific roles and responsibilities?

589. Who is responsible for each task?

590. Key conclusions and recommendations: Are conclusions and recommendations relevant and acceptable?

591. Who is involved?

592. Influence: what areas of organizational decision making are you able to influence when you do not have authority to make the final decision?

593. Authority: what areas/ISO 31000 projects in your

work do you have the authority to decide upon and act on the already stated decisions?

594. Do the values and practices inherent in the culture of your organization foster or hinder the process?

595. Once the responsibilities are defined for the ISO 31000 project, have the deliverables, roles and responsibilities been clearly communicated to every participant?

596. Does the team have access to and ability to use data analysis tools?

597. What should you highlight for improvement?

598. Required skills, knowledge, experience?

599. Was the expectation clearly communicated?

600. To decide whether to use a quality measurement, ask how will you know when it is achieved?

601. Are ISO 31000 project team roles and responsibilities identified and documented?

602. Are the quality assurance functions and related roles and responsibilities clearly defined?

2.29 Human Resource Management Plan: ISO 31000

603. What did you have to assume to be true to complete the charter?

604. Are tasks tracked by hours?

605. How to convince employees that this is a necessary process?

606. Is your organization primarily focused on a specific industry?

607. Have all involved ISO 31000 project stakeholders and work groups committed to the ISO 31000 project?

608. ISO 31000 project definition & scope?

609. List roles. what commitments have been made?

610. List the assumptions made to date. What did you have to assume to be true to complete the charter?

611. Are changes in scope (deliverable commitments) agreed to by all affected groups & individuals?

612. Has the ISO 31000 project manager been identified?

613. Quality of people required to meet the forecast needs of the department?

614. Has a ISO 31000 project Communications Plan been developed?

615. Has the schedule been baselined?

616. Has the business need been clearly defined?

617. What were things that you did well, and could improve, and how?

618. Does the ISO 31000 project have a Quality Culture?

619. Is your organization heading towards expansion, outsourcing of certain talents or making cut-backs to save money?

620. Identify who is needed on the core ISO 31000 project team to complete ISO 31000 project deliverables and achieve its goals and objectives. What skills, knowledge and experiences are required?

2.30 Communications Management Plan: ISO 31000

621. Do you prepare stakeholder engagement plans?

622. Who is the stakeholder?

623. What does the stakeholder need from the team?

624. Are stakeholders internal or external?

625. What to know?

626. Are others part of the communications management plan?

627. Who were proponents/opponents?

628. Why manage stakeholders?

629. Who did you turn to if you had questions?

630. Conflict resolution -which method when?

631. What is the political influence?

632. How do you manage communications?

633. Where do team members get information?

634. What is the stakeholders level of authority?

635. How much time does it take to do it?

636. Are others needed?

637. What is ISO 31000 project communications management?

638. How were corresponding initiatives successful?

639. Who will use or be affected by the result of a ISO 31000 project?

2.31 Risk Management Plan: ISO 31000

640. Premium on reliability of product?

641. Are the participants able to keep up with the workload?

642. Risks should be identified during which phase of ISO 31000 project management life cycle?

643. Have staff received necessary training?

644. Have top software and customer managers formally committed to support the ISO 31000 project?

645. Costs associated with late delivery or a defective product?

646. How is the audit profession changing?

647. Do the requirements require the creation of components that are unlike anything your organization has previously built?

648. What risks are necessary to achieve success?

649. Which is an input to the risk management process?

650. Financial risk: can your organization afford to undertake the ISO 31000 project?

651. Are the required plans included, such as nonstructural flood risk management plans?

652. Risk categories: what are the main categories of risks that should be addressed on this ISO 31000 project?

653. For software; does the software interface with new or unproven hardware or unproven vendor products?

654. Should the risk be taken at all?

655. Why do you want risk management?

656. Do you train all developers in the process?

657. Which risks should get the attention?

658. Where do risks appear in the business phases?

2.32 Risk Register: ISO 31000

659. Are there any knock-on effects/impact on any of the other areas?

660. What are you going to do to limit the ISO 31000 projects risk exposure due to the identified risks?

661. When is it going to be done?

662. Technology risk -is the ISO 31000 project technically feasible?

663. What are your key risks/show istoppers and what is being done to manage them?

664. Are implemented controls working as others should?

665. Cost/benefit – how much will the proposed mitigations cost and how does this cost compare with the potential cost of the risk event/situation should it occur?

666. What should you do now?

667. What may happen or not go according to plan?

668. Are your objectives at risk?

669. Why would you develop a risk register?

670. When would you develop a risk register?

671. What would the impact to the ISO 31000 project objectives be should the risk arise?

672. Market risk -will the new service or product be useful to your organization or marketable to others?

673. How are risks identified?

674. What risks might negatively or positively affect achieving the ISO 31000 project objectives?

675. Manageability – have mitigations to the risk been identified?

676. What could prevent you delivering on the strategic program objectives and what is being done to mitigate corresponding issues?

677. Have other controls and solutions been implemented in other services which could be applied as an alternative to additional funding?

678. What further options might be available for responding to the risk?

2.33 Probability and Impact Assessment: ISO 31000

679. Are the facilities, expertise, resources, and management know-how available to handle the situation?

680. Risk may be made during which step of risk management?

681. Is the technology to be built new to your organization?

682. Are ISO 31000 project requirements stable?

683. What should be the level of difficulty in handling the technology?

684. Who should be responsible for the monitoring and tracking of the indicators youhave identified?

685. What will be the environmental impact of the ISO 31000 project?

686. Do you use diagramming techniques to show cause and effect?

687. Is the number of people on the ISO 31000 project team adequate to do the job?

688. Do end-users have realistic expectations?

689. Why has this particular mode of contracting been

chosen?

690. What is the likelihood?

691. Do you have a consistent repeatable process that is actually used?

692. Which of corresponding risk factors can be avoided altogether?

693. Is the present organizational structure for handling the ISO 31000 project sufficient?

694. Does the software interface with new or unproven hardware or unproven vendor products?

695. How do risks change during a ISO 31000 project life cycle?

696. What are the uncertainties associated with the technology selected for the ISO 31000 project?

697. Is security a central objective?

698. What is the experience (performance, attitude, business ethics, etc.) in the past with contractors?

2.34 Probability and Impact Matrix: ISO 31000

699. My ISO 31000 project leader has suddenly left your organization, what do you do?

700. Which phase of the ISO 31000 project do you take part in?

701. What would be the effect of slippage?

702. Several experts are offsite, and wish to be included. How can this be done?

703. What should be the gestation period for the ISO 31000 project with this technology?

704. Are some people working on multiple ISO 31000 projects?

705. Can you handle the investment risk?

706. Can the ISO 31000 project proceed without assuming the risk?

707. What are the methods to deal with risks?

708. What are the probable external agencies to act as ISO 31000 project manager?

709. What new technologies are being explored in the same area?

710. What risks were tracked?

711. Has something like this been done before?

712. What are the likely future requirements?

713. How solid are the price-volume ISO 31000 projections?

714. What action do you usually take against risks?

2.35 Risk Data Sheet: ISO 31000

715. How can it happen?

716. What were the Causes that contributed?

717. How reliable is the data source?

718. Has a sensitivity analysis been carried out?

719. Type of risk identified?

720. How do you handle product safely?

721. What is the chance that it will happen?

722. What are you here for (Mission)?

723. What actions can be taken to eliminate or remove risk?

724. What are you trying to achieve (Objectives)?

725. Do effective diagnostic tests exist?

726. Who has a vested interest in how you perform as your organization (our stakeholders)?

727. Will revised controls lead to tolerable risk levels?

728. What can happen?

729. Risk of what?

730. What will be the consequences if it happens?

731. If it happens, what are the consequences?

732. Potential for recurrence?

733. What is the likelihood of it happening?

734. What was measured?

2.36 Procurement Management Plan: ISO 31000

735. Is the steering committee active in ISO 31000 project oversight?

736. Has the budget been baselined?

737. Is there a procurement management plan in place?

738. Are ISO 31000 project team roles and responsibilities identified and documented?

739. Are vendor invoices audited for accuracy before payment?

740. Is an industry recognized mechanized support tool(s) being used for ISO 31000 project scheduling & tracking?

741. Is there a formal set of procedures supporting Issues Management?

742. Have external dependencies been captured in the schedule?

743. Is there a set of procedures defining the scope, procedures, and deliverables defining quality control?

744. Staffing Requirements?

745. Has a structured approach been used to break

work effort into manageable components (WBS)?

746. Do all stakeholders know how to access the PM repository and where to find the ISO 31000 project documentation?

747. Is a pmo (ISO 31000 project management office) in place which provides oversight to the ISO 31000 project?

748. Are the budget estimates reasonable?

749. Are parking lot items captured?

750. Does the ISO 31000 project have a Statement of Work?

751. Were ISO 31000 project team members involved in the development of activity & task decomposition?

2.37 Source Selection Criteria: ISO 31000

752. How should comments received in response to a RFP be handled?

753. When and what information can be considered with offerors regarding past performance?

754. Are resultant proposal revisions allowed?

755. Who must be notified?

756. What should communications be used to accomplish?

757. Do you want to have them collaborate at subfactor level?

758. What common questions or problems are associated with debriefings?

759. Is this a cost contract?

760. What is the basis of an estimate and what assumptions were made?

761. Are considerations anticipated?

762. How organization are proposed quotes/prices?

763. What can not be disclosed?

764. How are oral presentations documented?

765. Can you reasonably estimate total organization requirements for the coming year?

766. What documentation is necessary regarding electronic communications?

767. What does an evaluation address and what does a sample resemble?

768. How do you encourage efficiency and consistency?

769. How long will it take for the purchase cost to be the same as the lease cost?

770. Who should attend debriefings?

771. Who is entitled to a debriefing?

2.38 Stakeholder Management Plan: ISO 31000

772. What potential impact does the ISO 31000 project have on the stakeholder?

773. Where does the information come from?

774. Are vendor contract reports, reviews and visits conducted periodically?

775. After observing execution of process, is it in compliance with the documented Plan?

776. Why would you develop a ISO 31000 project Execution Plan?

777. Are ISO 31000 project contact logs kept up to date?

778. What training requirements are there based upon the required skills and resources?

779. Are communication systems currently in place appropriate?

780. Contradictory information between document sections?

781. Is ISO 31000 project status reviewed with the steering and executive teams at appropriate intervals?

782. Are assumptions being identified, recorded,

analyzed, qualified and closed?

783. Which impacts could serve as impediments?

784. Are there standards for code development?

785. When would you develop a ISO 31000 project Business Plan?

786. Where to get additional help?

787. Is the communication plan being followed?

788. Has a resource management plan been created?

789. Is there an onboarding process in place?

2.39 Change Management Plan: ISO 31000

790. What provokes organizational change?

791. What will be the preferred method of delivery?

792. What are the major changes to processes?

793. What new roles are needed?

794. What relationships will change?

795. How does the principle of senders and receivers make the ISO 31000 project communications effort more complex?

796. Has the training provider been established?

797. What is the reason for the communication?

798. Who might be able to help you the most?

799. How frequently should you repeat the message?

800. What communication network would you use – informal or formal?

801. What processes are in place to manage knowledge about the ISO 31000 project?

802. What are the training strategies?

803. Is there support for this application(s) and are the details available for distribution?

804. What goal(s) do you hope to accomplish?

805. Will the culture embrace or reject this change?

806. Are there resource implications for your communications strategy?

807. What new behaviours are required?

808. What work practices will be affected?

3.0 Executing Process Group: ISO 31000

809. How many different communication channels does the ISO 31000 project team have?

810. How well defined and documented were the ISO 31000 project management processes you chose to use?

811. How is ISO 31000 project performance information created and distributed?

812. What were things that you need to improve?

813. What are the critical steps involved in selecting measures and initiatives?

814. What good practices or successful experiences or transferable examples have been identified?

815. What are deliverables of your ISO 31000 project?

816. Who will provide training?

817. Were sponsors and decision makers available when needed outside regularly scheduled meetings?

818. Have operating capacities been created and/or reinforced in partners?

819. How could stakeholders negatively impact your ISO 31000 project?

820. Who will be the main sponsor?

821. How do you enter durations, link tasks, and view critical path information?

822. How could you control progress of your ISO 31000 project?

823. Do ISO 31000 project managers understand your organizational context for ISO 31000 projects?

824. Is the program supported by national and/or local organizations?

825. Just how important is your work to the overall success of the ISO 31000 project?

3.1 Team Member Status Report: ISO 31000

826. How can you make it practical?

827. Are your organizations ISO 31000 projects more successful over time?

828. How will resource planning be done?

829. How does this product, good, or service meet the needs of the ISO 31000 project and your organization as a whole?

830. Does every department have to have a ISO 31000 project Manager on staff?

831. What is to be done?

832. How much risk is involved?

833. When a teams productivity and success depend on collaboration and the efficient flow of information, what generally fails them?

834. How it is to be done?

835. Are the products of your organizations ISO 31000 projects meeting customers objectives?

836. Does the product, good, or service already exist within your organization?

837. What specific interest groups do you have in place?

838. Is there evidence that staff is taking a more professional approach toward management of your organizations ISO 31000 projects?

839. Will the staff do training or is that done by a third party?

840. Do you have an Enterprise ISO 31000 project Management Office (EPMO)?

841. Are the attitudes of staff regarding ISO 31000 project work improving?

842. Why is it to be done?

843. Does your organization have the means (staff, money, contract, etc.) to produce or to acquire the product, good, or service?

844. The problem with Reward & Recognition Programs is that the truly deserving people all too often get left out. How can you make it practical?

3.2 Change Request: ISO 31000

845. Who is communicating the change?

846. Change request coordination ?

847. How is quality being addressed on the ISO 31000 project?

848. How are changes graded and who is responsible for the rating?

849. What are the requirements for urgent changes?

850. Who is included in the change control team?

851. Customer acceptance plan how will the customer verify the change has been implemented successfully?

852. Will the change use memory to the extent that other functions will be not have sufficient memory to operate effectively?

853. Who is responsible for the implementation and monitoring of all measures?

854. Screen shots or attachments included in a Change Request?

855. Can you answer what happened, who did it, when did it happen, and what else will be affected?

856. How shall the implementation of changes be

recorded?

857. For which areas does this operating procedure apply?

858. Has the change been highlighted and documented in the CSCI?

859. What should be regulated in a change control operating instruction?

860. How is the change documented (format, content, storage)?

861. Who can suggest changes?

862. Who will perform the change?

863. Will all change requests be unconditionally tracked through this process?

3.3 Change Log: ISO 31000

864. How does this change affect the timeline of the schedule?

865. Is the change request within ISO 31000 project scope?

866. When was the request approved?

867. How does this relate to the standards developed for specific business processes?

868. Is the requested change request a result of changes in other ISO 31000 project(s)?

869. Is the change request open, closed or pending?

870. How does this change affect scope?

871. Do the described changes impact on the integrity or security of the system?

872. Who initiated the change request?

873. Is the change backward compatible without limitations?

874. Where do changes come from?

875. Is this a mandatory replacement?

876. Is the submitted change a new change or a modification of a previously approved change?

877. When was the request submitted?

878. Will the ISO 31000 project fail if the change request is not executed?

3.4 Decision Log: ISO 31000

879. Is everything working as expected?

880. How consolidated and comprehensive a story can you tell by capturing currently available incident data in a central location and through a log of key decisions during an incident?

881. How effective is maintaining the log at facilitating organizational learning?

882. Adversarial environment. is your opponent open to a non-traditional workflow, or will it likely challenge anything you do?

883. At what point in time does loss become unacceptable?

884. How do you define success?

885. How does the use a Decision Support System influence the strategies/tactics or costs?

886. What eDiscovery problem or issue did your organization set out to fix or make better?

887. Decision-making process; how will the team make decisions?

888. Linked to original objective?

889. Who is the decisionmaker?

890. Do strategies and tactics aimed at less than full control reduce the costs of management or simply shift the cost burden?

891. Who will be given a copy of this document and where will it be kept?

892. What is your overall strategy for quality control / quality assurance procedures?

893. What is the average size of your matters in an applicable measurement?

894. How does provision of information, both in terms of content and presentation, influence acceptance of alternative strategies?

895. Which variables make a critical difference?

896. With whom was the decision shared or considered?

897. It becomes critical to track and periodically revisit both operational effectiveness; Are you noticing all that you need to, and are you interpreting what you see effectively?

898. What was the rationale for the decision?

3.5 Quality Audit: ISO 31000

899. How does your organization know that its research planning and management systems are appropriately effective and constructive in enabling quality research outcomes?

900. How does your organization know that the research supervision provided to its staff is appropriately effective and constructive?

901. Are training programs documented?

902. How does your organization know that its financial management system is appropriately effective and constructive?

903. How does your organization know that its Governance system is appropriately effective and constructive?

904. How does your organization know that its staff financial services are appropriately effective and constructive?

905. Are all records associated with the reconditioning of a device maintained for a minimum of two years after the sale or disposal of the last device within a lot of merchandise?

906. Are multiple statements on the same issue consistent with each other?

907. What does an analysis of your organizations staff

profile suggest in terms of its planning, and how is this being addressed?

908. How does your organization know that its range of activities are being reviewed as rigorously and constructively as they could be?

909. Are all employees including salespersons made aware that they must report all complaints received from any source for inclusion in the complaint handling system?

910. How does your organization know that its advisory services are appropriately effective and constructive?

911. How does your organization know that it is effectively and constructively guiding staff through to timely completion of tasks?

912. Does the report read coherently?

913. How do you indicate the extent to which your personnel would be expected to contribute to the work effort?

914. What has changed/improved as a result of the review processes?

915. How does your organization know that its staff support services planning and management systems are appropriately effective and constructive?

916. How does your organization know that its staff placements are appropriately effective and constructive in relation to program-related learning

outcomes?

917. How does your organization know that its relationships with industry and employers are appropriately effective and constructive?

918. Is there a written corporate quality policy?

3.6 Team Directory: ISO 31000

919. Where should the information be distributed?

920. Process decisions: do invoice amounts match accepted work in place?

921. Why is the work necessary?

922. How will you accomplish and manage the objectives?

923. How does the team resolve conflicts and ensure tasks are completed?

924. Process decisions: are contractors adequately prosecuting the work?

925. Who will report ISO 31000 project status to all stakeholders?

926. Where will the product be used and/or delivered or built when appropriate?

927. Days from the time the issue is identified?

928. Have you decided when to celebrate the ISO 31000 projects completion date?

929. Contract requirements complied with?

930. Who are your stakeholders (customers, sponsors, end users, team members)?

931. When does information need to be distributed?

932. Decisions: what could be done better to improve the quality of the constructed product?

933. Who should receive information (all stakeholders)?

934. How and in what format should information be presented?

935. Who is the Sponsor?

936. When will you produce deliverables?

937. Process decisions: are there any statutory or regulatory issues relevant to the timely execution of work?

3.7 Team Operating Agreement: ISO 31000

938. Are leadership responsibilities shared among team members (versus a single leader)?

939. Do team members need to frequently communicate as a full group to make timely decisions?

940. Did you draft the meeting agenda?

941. Did you recap the meeting purpose, time, and expectations?

942. What is the anticipated procedure (recruitment, solicitation of volunteers, or assignment) for selecting team members?

943. What are the safety issues/risks that need to be addressed and/or that the team needs to consider?

944. Do you listen for voice tone and word choice to understand the meaning behind words?

945. Has the appropriate access to relevant data and analysis capability been granted?

946. Have you established procedures that team members can follow to work effectively together, such as a team operating agreement?

947. Confidentiality: how will confidential information

be handled?

948. How do you want to be thought of and known within your organization?

949. To whom do you deliver your services?

950. Seconds for members to respond?

951. What types of accommodations will be formulated and put in place for sustaining the team?

952. Do you begin with a question to engage everyone?

953. Do you call or email participants to ensure understanding, follow-through and commitment to the meeting outcomes?

954. Are there the right people on your team?

955. Did you prepare participants for the next meeting?

956. Have you set the goals and objectives of the team?

3.8 Team Performance Assessment: ISO 31000

957. To what degree are corresponding categories of skills either actually or potentially represented across the membership?

958. How hard do you try to make a good selection?

959. To what degree are the goals ambitious?

960. To what degree is the team cognizant of small wins to be celebrated along the way?

961. To what degree will the approach capitalize on and enhance the skills of all team members in a manner that takes into consideration other demands on members of the team?

962. To what degree are fresh input and perspectives systematically caught and added (for example, through information and analysis, new members, and senior sponsors)?

963. Where to from here?

964. What makes opportunities more or less obvious?

965. To what degree does the teams work approach provide opportunity for members to engage in fact-based problem solving?

966. To what degree do team members frequently

explore the teams purpose and its implications?

967. How does ISO 31000 project termination impact ISO 31000 project team members?

968. To what degree will new and supplemental skills be introduced as the need is recognized?

969. When a reviewer complains about method variance, what is the essence of the complaint?

970. Does more radicalness mean more perceived benefits?

971. To what degree does the teams approach to its work allow for modification and improvement over time?

972. Delaying market entry: how long is too long?

973. How do you encourage members to learn from each other?

974. Lack of method variance in self-reported affect and perceptions at work: Reality or artifact?

975. To what degree are the teams goals and objectives clear, simple, and measurable?

3.9 Team Member Performance Assessment: ISO 31000

976. To what degree does the teams purpose contain themes that are particularly meaningful and memorable?

977. How do you know that all team members are learning?

978. What instructional strategies were developed/ incorporated (e.g., direct instruction, indirect instruction, experiential learning, independent study, interactive instruction)?

979. Are the goals SMART ?

980. How do you make use of research?

981. What variables that affect team members achievement are within your control?

982. What qualities does a successful Team leader possess?

983. For what period of time is a member rated?

984. Who receives a benchmark visit?

985. To what degree does the team possess adequate membership to achieve its ends?

986. What are the evaluation strategies (e.g., reaction,

learning, behavior, results) used. What evaluation results did you have?

987. To what degree do team members understand one anothers roles and skills?

988. To what extent did the evaluation influence the instructional path, such as with adaptive testing?

989. Who they are?

990. Are the draft goals SMART ?

991. Which training platform formats (i.e., mobile, virtual, videogame-based) were implemented in your effort(s)?

992. How are performance measures and associated incentives developed?

993. How do you determine which data are the most important to use, analyze, or review?

3.10 Issue Log: ISO 31000

994. What steps can you take for positive relationships?

995. Who do you turn to if you have questions?

996. Why do you manage communications?

997. Which stakeholders can influence others?

998. Do you have members of your team responsible for certain stakeholders?

999. Is the issue log kept in a safe place?

1000. Are there potential barriers between the team and the stakeholder?

1001. How do you manage human resources?

1002. What is the status of the issue?

1003. What approaches to you feel are the best ones to use?

1004. Persistence; will users learn a work around or will they be bothered every time?

1005. Are they needed?

1006. What is a Stakeholder?

1007. What approaches do you use?

1008. Are the ISO 31000 project issues uniquely identified, including to which product they refer?

1009. Why multiple evaluators?

4.0 Monitoring and Controlling Process Group: ISO 31000

1010. Is there sufficient funding available for this?

1011. Is progress on outcomes due to your program?

1012. What resources (both financial and non-financial) are available/needed?

1013. Measurable - are the targets measurable?

1014. What do they need to know about the ISO 31000 project?

1015. How were collaborations developed, and how are they sustained?

1016. How is agile program management done?

1017. When will the ISO 31000 project be done?

1018. What input will you be required to provide the ISO 31000 project team?

1019. Change, where should you look for problems?

1020. How is agile ISO 31000 project management done?

1021. Purpose: toward what end is the evaluation being conducted?

1022. Does the solution fit in with organizations technical architectural requirements?

1023. Did the ISO 31000 project team have enough people to execute the ISO 31000 project plan?

1024. How is agile portfolio management done?

1025. Contingency planning. if a risk event occurs, what will you do?

4.1 Project Performance Report: ISO 31000

1026. To what degree are the goals realistic?

1027. To what degree does the funding match the requirement?

1028. To what degree are the members clear on what they are individually responsible for and what they are jointly responsible for?

1029. What is the PRS?

1030. To what degree does the teams work approach provide opportunity for members to engage in results-based evaluation?

1031. To what degree do all members feel responsible for all agreed-upon measures?

1032. How will procurement be coordinated with other ISO 31000 project aspects, such as scheduling and performance reporting?

1033. To what degree are the skill areas critical to team performance present?

1034. To what degree are the demands of the task compatible with and converge with the relationships of the informal organization?

1035. What is in it for you?

1036. To what degree does the teams work approach provide opportunity for members to engage in open interaction?

1037. To what degree is there a sense that only the team can succeed?

1038. To what degree is there centralized control of information sharing?

1039. To what degree can the cognitive capacity of individuals accommodate the flow of information?

1040. Next Steps?

1041. To what degree is the information network consistent with the structure of the formal organization?

1042. What is the degree to which rules govern information exchange between individuals within your organization?

4.2 Variance Analysis: ISO 31000

1043. When, during the last four quarters, did a primary business event occur causing a fluctuation?

1044. Are the actual costs used for variance analysis reconcilable with data from the accounting system?

1045. How do you evaluate the impact of schedule changes, work around, et?

1046. What is the budgeted cost for work scheduled?

1047. What does an unfavorable overhead volume variance mean?

1048. How do you identify potential or actual overruns and underruns?

1049. Can the contractor substantiate work package and planning package budgets?

1050. Are overhead cost budgets established for each department which has authority to incur overhead costs?

1051. Can the relationship with problem customers be restructured so that there is a win-win situation?

1052. Do the rates and prices remain constant throughout the year?

1053. Budget versus actual. how does the monthly budget compare to actual experience?

1054. What should management do?

1055. Is the market likely to continue to grow at this rate next year?

1056. Does the contractors system identify work accomplishment against the schedule plan?

1057. Are procedures for variance analysis documented and consistently applied at the control account level and selected WBS and organizational levels at least monthly as a routine task?

1058. Wbs elements contractually specified for reporting of status to your organization (lowest level only)?

1059. Did a new competitor enter the market?

1060. Who are responsible for overhead performance control of related costs?

4.3 Earned Value Status: ISO 31000

1061. Earned value can be used in almost any ISO 31000 project situation and in almost any ISO 31000 project environment. it may be used on large ISO 31000 projects, medium sized ISO 31000 projects, tiny ISO 31000 projects (in cut-down form), complex and simple ISO 31000 projects and in any market sector. some people, of course, know all about earned value, they have used it for years - but perhaps not as effectively as they could have?

1062. Where are your problem areas?

1063. Validation is a process of ensuring that the developed system will actually achieve the stakeholders desired outcomes; Are you building the right product? What do you validate?

1064. Are you hitting your ISO 31000 projects targets?

1065. How much is it going to cost by the finish?

1066. How does this compare with other ISO 31000 projects?

1067. Where is evidence-based earned value in your organization reported?

1068. If earned value management (EVM) is so good in determining the true status of a ISO 31000 project and ISO 31000 project its completion, why is it that hardly any one uses it in information systems related ISO 31000 projects?

1069. When is it going to finish?

1070. Verification is a process of ensuring that the developed system satisfies the stakeholders agreements and specifications; Are you building the product right? What do you verify?

1071. What is the unit of forecast value?

4.4 Risk Audit: ISO 31000

1072. Improving fraud detection: do auditors react to abnormal inconsistencies between financial and non-financial measures?

1073. Does your organization have a process for meeting its ongoing taxation obligations?

1074. Have risks been considered with an insurance broker or provider and suitable insurance cover been arranged?

1075. What does monitoring consist of?

1076. Are the best people available?

1077. Do you have an understanding of insurance claims processes?

1078. Do you record and file all audits?

1079. Are risk assessments documented?

1080. If applicable; which route/packaging option do you choose for transport of hazmat material?

1081. Are tool mentors available?

1082. Have you considered the health and safety of everyone in your organization and do you meet work health and safety regulations?

1083. Who is responsible for what?

1084. What is the effect of globalisation; is business becoming too complex and can the auditor rely on auditing standards?

1085. Are all managers or operators of the facility or equipment competent or qualified?

1086. Will safety checks of personal equipment supplied by competitors be conducted?

1087. Estimated size of product in number of programs, files, transactions?

1088. Are auditors able to effectively apply more soft evidence found in the risk-assessment process with the results of more tangible audit evidence found through more substantive testing?

1089. How risk averse are you?

1090. Do you promote education and training opportunities?

1091. Have all possible risks/hazards been identified (including injury to staff, damage to equipment, impact on others in the community)?

4.5 Contractor Status Report: ISO 31000

1092. What is the average response time for answering a support call?

1093. What are the minimum and optimal bandwidth requirements for the proposed solution?

1094. What process manages the contracts?

1095. How does the proposed individual meet each requirement?

1096. Who can list a ISO 31000 project as organization experience, your organization or a previous employee of your organization?

1097. What was the final actual cost?

1098. How is risk transferred?

1099. How long have you been using the services?

1100. If applicable; describe your standard schedule for new software version releases. Are new software version releases included in the standard maintenance plan?

1101. What was the budget or estimated cost for your organizations services?

1102. Describe how often regular updates are made

to the proposed solution. Are corresponding regular updates included in the standard maintenance plan?

1103. What was the overall budget or estimated cost?

1104. Are there contractual transfer concerns?

1105. What was the actual budget or estimated cost for your organizations services?

4.6 Formal Acceptance: ISO 31000

1106. Do you buy-in installation services?

1107. What are the requirements against which to test, Who will execute?

1108. Was the ISO 31000 project managed well?

1109. Have all comments been addressed?

1110. Does it do what ISO 31000 project team said it would?

1111. Was the ISO 31000 project work done on time, within budget, and according to specification?

1112. How does your team plan to obtain formal acceptance on your ISO 31000 project?

1113. What can you do better next time?

1114. Do you buy pre-configured systems or build your own configuration?

1115. Who supplies data?

1116. Do you perform formal acceptance or burn-in tests?

1117. What features, practices, and processes proved to be strengths or weaknesses?

1118. What is the Acceptance Management Process?

1119. Did the ISO 31000 project achieve its MOV?

1120. Is formal acceptance of the ISO 31000 project product documented and distributed?

1121. Was the sponsor/customer satisfied?

1122. What lessons were learned about your ISO 31000 project management methodology?

1123. General estimate of the costs and times to complete the ISO 31000 project?

1124. Was the client satisfied with the ISO 31000 project results?

1125. What function(s) does it fill or meet?

5.0 Closing Process Group: ISO 31000

1126. Were risks identified and mitigated?

1127. What is the risk of failure to your organization?

1128. How well defined and documented were the ISO 31000 project management processes you chose to use?

1129. What will you do to minimize the impact should a risk event occur?

1130. Is the ISO 31000 project funded?

1131. What is the amount of funding and what ISO 31000 project phases are funded?

1132. What were things that you did very well and want to do the same again on the next ISO 31000 project?

1133. Is this a follow-on to a previous ISO 31000 project?

1134. How will you know you did it?

1135. Is this an updated ISO 31000 project Proposal Document?

1136. If a risk event occurs, what will you do?

1137. Did you do what you said you were going to do?

1138. What can you do better next time, and what specific actions can you take to improve?

1139. What were the desired outcomes?

1140. What could have been improved?

1141. Does the close educate others to improve performance?

1142. What do you need to do?

5.1 Procurement Audit: ISO 31000

1143. Is the minutes book kept current?

1144. Are cases of double payment duly prevented and corrected?

1145. Are there reasonable procedures to identify possible sources of supply?

1146. Are the supporting documents for payments voided or cancelled following payment?

1147. Is there a purchasing policy as to the amount of an order on which bidding is required?

1148. Is your organization aware and informed about international procurement standards and good practice?

1149. Were additional works strictly necessary for the completion of performance under the contract?

1150. Are rules in automatic disbursement programs adequate to prevent duplicate payment of invoices?

1151. Is there a procedure on requesting bids?

1152. Were calculations used in evaluation adequate and correct?

1153. Has your organization clearly defined the award criteria?

1154. Are internal control systems in place?

1155. Was the outcome of the award process properly reached and communicated?

1156. Have guidelines been set up for how the procurement process should be conducted?

1157. When performance conditions were detailed in the tender documentation, did the contracting authority verify if the tenders received met the already stated requirements?

1158. Did the contracting authority offer unrestricted and full electronic access to the contract documents and any supplementary documents (specifying the internet address in the notice)?

1159. Is there no evidence of collusion between bidders?

1160. Are regulations and protective measures in place to avoid corruption?

1161. Was invitation to tender to each specific contract issued after the evaluation of the indicative tenders was completed?

1162. Were results of the award procedures published?

5.2 Contract Close-Out: ISO 31000

1163. Parties: who is involved?

1164. Have all contracts been completed?

1165. How does it work?

1166. Have all contracts been closed?

1167. Was the contract type appropriate?

1168. Has each contract been audited to verify acceptance and delivery?

1169. What happens to the recipient of services?

1170. What is capture management?

1171. Change in attitude or behavior?

1172. Have all contract records been included in the ISO 31000 project archives?

1173. Was the contract complete without requiring numerous changes and revisions?

1174. How is the contracting office notified of the automatic contract close-out?

1175. Have all acceptance criteria been met prior to final payment to contractors?

1176. Change in knowledge?

1177. Change in circumstances?

1178. Are the signers the authorized officials?

1179. How/when used ?

1180. Was the contract sufficiently clear so as not to result in numerous disputes and misunderstandings?

1181. Parties: Authorized?

5.3 Project or Phase Close-Out: ISO 31000

1182. What is a Risk?

1183. Complete yes or no?

1184. Have business partners been involved extensively, and what data was required for them?

1185. What is a Risk Management Process?

1186. What is the information level of detail required for each stakeholder?

1187. Were the outcomes different from the already stated planned?

1188. Were messages directly related to the release strategy or phases of the ISO 31000 project?

1189. What are the mandatory communication needs for each stakeholder?

1190. What is this stakeholder expecting?

1191. If you were the ISO 31000 project sponsor, how would you determine which ISO 31000 project team(s) and/or individuals deserve recognition?

1192. In preparing the Lessons Learned report, should it reflect a consensus viewpoint, or should the report reflect the different individual viewpoints?

1193. Can the lesson learned be replicated?

1194. Does the lesson educate others to improve performance?

1195. Who are the ISO 31000 project stakeholders and what are roles and involvement?

1196. Planned remaining costs?

1197. Who controlled the resources for the ISO 31000 project?

1198. Who is responsible for award close-out?

1199. Were cost budgets met?

1200. Is the lesson significant, valid, and applicable?

5.4 Lessons Learned: ISO 31000

1201. What is the growth stage of your organization?

1202. What is the distribution of authority?

1203. What regulatory constraints impact the case?

1204. What is the frequency of group communications?

1205. What needs to be done over or differently?

1206. What worked well/did not work well?

1207. If you had to do this ISO 31000 project again, what is the one thing that you would change (related to process, not to technical solutions)?

1208. How does the budget cycle affect the case?

1209. How often did you violate the rules?

1210. What is the frequency of communication?

1211. Would you spend your own money to fix this issue?

1212. How well did the scope of the ISO 31000 project match what was defined in the ISO 31000 project Proposal?

1213. What specialization does the task require?

1214. What are the needs of the individuals?

1215. How useful was the content of the training you received in preparation for the use of the product/ service?

1216. How was the political and social history changed over the life of the ISO 31000 project?

1217. How satisfied are you with your involvement in the development and/or review of the ISO 31000 project Scope during ISO 31000 project Initiation and Planning?

1218. How effectively and timely was your organizational change impact identified and planned for?

1219. What is the impact of tax policy on the case?

1220. To what extent was the evolution of risks communicated?

ISO 31000 and Managing Projects, Criteria for Project Managers:

1.0 Initiating Process Group: ISO 31000

1. Information sharing?

2. How well defined and documented were the ISO 31000 project management processes you chose to use?

3. Did you use a contractor or vendor?

4. In which ISO 31000 project management process group is the detailed ISO 31000 project budget created?

5. What business situation is being addressed?

6. If the risk event occurs, what will you do?

7. At which stage, in a typical ISO 31000 project do stake holders have maximum influence?

8. What will be the pressing issues of tomorrow?

9. Were decisions made in a timely manner?

10. What communication items need improvement?

11. Were escalated issues resolved promptly?

12. Contingency planning. if a risk event occurs, what will you do?

13. Do you understand all business (operational), technical, resource and vendor risks associated with

the ISO 31000 project?

14. During which stage of Risk planning are modeling techniques used to determine overall effects of risks on ISO 31000 project objectives for high probability, high impact risks?

15. Who is involved in each phase?

16. Are the ISO 31000 project team and stakeholders meeting regularly and using a meeting agenda and taking notes to accurately document what is being covered and what happened in the weekly meetings?

17. How well did the chosen processes fit the needs of the ISO 31000 project?

18. The ISO 31000 project you are managing has nine stakeholders. How many channel of communications are there between corresponding stakeholders?

19. Do you know if the ISO 31000 project requires outside equipment or vendor resources?

20. Who is performing the work of the ISO 31000 project?

1.1 Project Charter: ISO 31000

21. Why do you need to manage scope?

22. How will you know a change is an improvement?

23. Where does all this information come from?

24. Environmental stewardship and sustainability considerations: what is the process that will be used to ensure compliance with the environmental stewardship policy?

25. What barriers do you predict to your success?

26. Who will take notes, document decisions?

27. Fit with other Products Compliments – Cannibalizes?

28. Are you building in-house ?

29. When do you use a ISO 31000 project Charter?

30. What material?

31. What is the most common tool for helping define the detail?

32. Why Outsource?

33. Customer benefits: what customer requirements does this ISO 31000 project address?

34. What are the assumptions?

35. When is a charter needed?

36. Why have you chosen the aim you have set forth?

37. Pop quiz – which are the same inputs as in the ISO 31000 project charter?

38. What is in it for you?

39. What are you trying to accomplish?

40. Review the general mission What system will be affected by the improvement efforts?

1.2 Stakeholder Register: ISO 31000

41. Who are the stakeholders?

42. How will reports be created?

43. Who is managing stakeholder engagement?

44. How should employers make voices heard?

45. What opportunities exist to provide communications?

46. What is the power of the stakeholder?

47. Is your organization ready for change?

48. What & Why?

49. How much influence do they have on the ISO 31000 project?

50. What are the major ISO 31000 project milestones requiring communications or providing communications opportunities?

51. Who wants to talk about Security?

52. How big is the gap?

1.3 Stakeholder Analysis Matrix: ISO 31000

53. What is the stakeholders name, what is function?

54. Insurmountable weaknesses?

55. How do rules, behaviors affect stakes?

56. Effects on core activities, distraction?

57. How do customers express needs?

58. Who holds positions of responsibility in interested organizations?

59. What is the stakeholders mandate, what is mission?

60. Is there a clear description of the scope of practice of the ISO 31000 projects educators?

61. Which conditions out of the control of the management are crucial for the sustainability of its effects?

62. What tools would help you communicate?

63. Which conditions out of the control of the management are crucial to contribute for the achievement of the development objective?

64. What resources might the stakeholder bring to the

ISO 31000 project?

65. Political effects?

66. How much do resources cost?

67. What coalitions might build around the issues being tackled?

68. Niche target markets?

69. What is your Advocacy Strategy?

70. How will the ISO 31000 project benefit them?

71. Environmental effects?

72. Processes, systems, it, communications?

2.0 Planning Process Group: ISO 31000

73. How many days can task X be late in starting without affecting the ISO 31000 project completion date?

74. Product breakdown structure (pbs): what is the ISO 31000 project result or product, and how should it look like, what are its parts?

75. How well did the chosen processes fit the needs of the ISO 31000 project?

76. Who are the ISO 31000 project stakeholders?

77. How do you integrate ISO 31000 project Planning with the Iterative/Evolutionary SDLC?

78. To what extent are the participating departments coordinating with each other?

79. If task x starts two days late, what is the effect on the ISO 31000 project end date?

80. If you are late, will anybody notice?

81. What will you do?

82. In what way has the program contributed towards the issue culture and development included on the public agenda?

83. How will you do it?

84. How well do the team follow the chosen processes?

85. What types of differentiated effects are resulting from the ISO 31000 project and to what extent?

86. Are you just doing busywork to pass the time?

87. Is the ISO 31000 project making progress in helping to achieve the set results?

88. You did your readings, yes?

89. What factors are contributing to progress or delay in the achievement of products and results?

90. How well defined and documented are the ISO 31000 project management processes you chose to use?

91. Why is it important to determine activity sequencing on ISO 31000 projects?

2.1 Project Management Plan: ISO 31000

92. What would you do differently?

93. How do you manage integration?

94. What is ISO 31000 project scope management?

95. Are there any Client staffing expectations?

96. Is mitigation authorized or recommended?

97. Are there any windfall benefits that would accrue to the ISO 31000 project sponsor or other parties?

98. What went wrong?

99. What are the known stakeholder requirements?

100. How well are you able to manage your risk?

101. What are the constraints?

102. What went right?

103. Who is the sponsor?

104. What are the assigned resources?

105. What worked well?

106. What data/reports/tools/etc. do program

managers need?

107. Are the proposed ISO 31000 project purposes different than a previously authorized ISO 31000 project?

108. Is there anything you would now do differently on your ISO 31000 project based on past experience?

2.2 Scope Management Plan: ISO 31000

109. Why is a scope management plan important?

110. Are decisions captured in a decisions log?

111. Have all involved ISO 31000 project stakeholders and work groups committed to the ISO 31000 project?

112. What are the risks that could significantly affect the communication on the ISO 31000 project?

113. Has adequate time for orientation & training of ISO 31000 project staff been provided for in relation to technical nature of the application and the experience levels of ISO 31000 project personnel?

114. Were ISO 31000 project team members involved in the development of activity & task decomposition?

115. Does the business case include how the ISO 31000 project aligns with your organizations strategic goals & objectives?

116. What is the need the ISO 31000 project will address?

117. Deliverables -are the deliverables tangible and verifiable?

118. What do you need to do to accomplish the goal or goals?

119. Are milestone deliverables effectively tracked and compared to ISO 31000 project plan?

120. To whom will the deliverables be first presented for inspection and verification?

121. What strengths do you have?

122. Do ISO 31000 project managers participating in the ISO 31000 project know the ISO 31000 projects true status first hand?

123. Are meeting objectives identified for each meeting?

124. How do you know when you are finished?

125. During what part of the PM process is the ISO 31000 project scope statement created?

126. Describe the process for rejecting the ISO 31000 project deliverables. What happens to rejected deliverables?

127. Have stakeholder accountabilities & responsibilities been clearly defined?

128. Is there a formal process for updating the ISO 31000 project baseline?

2.3 Requirements Management Plan: ISO 31000

129. Do you have an agreed upon process for alerting the ISO 31000 project Manager if a request for change in requirements leads to a product scope change?

130. Will you have access to stakeholders when you need them?

131. Should you include sub-activities?

132. Are actual resources expenditures versus planned expenditures acceptable?

133. Is any organizational data being used or stored?

134. How do you know that you have done this right?

135. Controlling ISO 31000 project requirements involves monitoring the status of the ISO 31000 project requirements and managing changes to the requirements. Who is responsible for monitoring and tracking the ISO 31000 project requirements?

136. Will you document changes to requirements?

137. Who is responsible for monitoring and tracking the ISO 31000 project requirements?

138. What cost metrics will be used?

139. Who will initially review the ISO 31000 project

work or products to ensure it meets the applicable acceptance criteria?

140. Is the user satisfied?

141. Is infrastructure setup part of your ISO 31000 project?

142. Is there formal agreement on who has authority to request a change in requirements?

143. Who came up with this requirement?

144. How will you develop the schedule of requirements activities?

145. How knowledgeable is the team in the proposed application area?

146. Do you expect stakeholders to be cooperative?

2.4 Requirements Documentation: ISO 31000

147. What facilities must be supported by the system?

148. What are current process problems?

149. What marketing channels do you want to use: e-mail, letter or sms?

150. Do your constraints stand?

151. What is effective documentation?

152. What if the system wasn t implemented?

153. Do technical resources exist?

154. What are the potential disadvantages/ advantages?

155. What will be the integration problems?

156. Can the requirement be changed without a large impact on other requirements?

157. How will the proposed ISO 31000 project help?

158. How will requirements be documented and who signs off on them?

159. If applicable; are there issues linked with the fact that this is an offshore ISO 31000 project?

160. How can you document system requirements?

161. Have the benefits identified with the system being identified clearly?

162. The problem with gathering requirements is right there in the word gathering. What images does it conjure?

163. What are the acceptance criteria?

164. Has requirements gathering uncovered information that would necessitate changes?

165. What is the risk associated with cost and schedule?

166. Who is involved?

2.5 Requirements Traceability Matrix: ISO 31000

167. What are the chronologies, contingencies, consequences, criteria?

168. What percentage of ISO 31000 projects are producing traceability matrices between requirements and other work products?

169. Why do you manage scope?

170. Describe the process for approving requirements so they can be added to the traceability matrix and ISO 31000 project work can be performed. Will the ISO 31000 project requirements become approved in writing?

171. Why use a WBS?

172. What is the WBS?

173. Will you use a Requirements Traceability Matrix?

174. How do you manage scope?

175. How small is small enough?

176. Is there a requirements traceability process in place?

177. How will it affect the stakeholders personally in career?

178. Do you have a clear understanding of all subcontracts in place?

2.6 Project Scope Statement: ISO 31000

179. Will all tasks resulting from issues be entered into the ISO 31000 project Plan and tracked through the plan?

180. Identify how your team and you will create the ISO 31000 project scope statement and the work breakdown structure (WBS). Document how you will create the ISO 31000 project scope statement and WBS, and make sure you answer the following questions: In defining ISO 31000 project scope and the WBS, will you and your ISO 31000 project team be using methods defined by your organization, methods defined by the ISO 31000 project management office (PMO), or other methods?

181. Is your organization structure appropriate for the ISO 31000 projects size and complexity?

182. If the scope changes, what will the impact be to your ISO 31000 project in terms of duration, cost, quality, or any other important areas of the ISO 31000 project?

183. Will the qa related information be reported regularly as part of the status reporting mechanisms?

184. Will statistics related to QA be collected, trends analyzed, and problems raised as issues?

185. Any new risks introduced or old risks impacted.

Are there issues that could affect the existing requirements for the result, service, or product if the scope changes?

186. What is a process you might recommend to verify the accuracy of the research deliverable?

187. Risks?

188. Has a method and process for requirement tracking been developed?

189. Which risks does the ISO 31000 project focus on?

190. Are the meetings set up to have assigned note takers that will add action/issues to the issue list?

191. What is change?

192. Is the plan under configuration management?

193. Will this process be communicated to the customer and ISO 31000 project team?

194. Who will you recommend approve the change, and when do you recommend the change reviews occur?

195. What should you drop in order to add something new?

196. Will the risk documents be filed?

197. Is there a process (test plans, inspections, reviews) defined for verifying outputs for each task?

198. Will the risk plan be updated on a regular and frequent basis?

2.7 Assumption and Constraint Log: ISO 31000

199. Are processes for release management of new development from coding and unit testing, to integration testing, to training, and production defined and followed?

200. What do you audit?

201. How do you design an auditing system?

202. Is the steering committee active in ISO 31000 project oversight?

203. Diagrams and tables are included to account for complex concepts and increase overall readability?

204. Would known impacts serve as impediments?

205. What do you log?

206. Is there documentation of system capability requirements, data requirements, environment requirements, security requirements, and computer and hardware requirements?

207. Are formal code reviews conducted?

208. Should factors be unpredictable over time?

209. How relevant is this attribute to this ISO 31000 project or audit?

210. Are best practices and metrics employed to identify issues, progress, performance, etc.?

211. Is there adequate stakeholder participation for the vetting of requirements definition, changes and management?

212. Can the requirements be traced to the appropriate components of the solution, as well as test scripts?

213. Security analysis has access to information that is sanitized?

214. Violation trace: why ?

215. Are there nonconformance issues?

216. Does the document/deliverable meet all requirements (for example, statement of work) specific to this deliverable?

217. Does a specific action and/or state that is known to violate security policy occur?

2.8 Work Breakdown Structure: ISO 31000

218. When does it have to be done?

219. Is it still viable?

220. Is it a change in scope?

221. When do you stop?

222. Why would you develop a Work Breakdown Structure?

223. Can you make it?

224. How will you and your ISO 31000 project team define the ISO 31000 projects scope and work breakdown structure?

225. What is the probability that the ISO 31000 project duration will exceed xx weeks?

226. Is the work breakdown structure (wbs) defined and is the scope of the ISO 31000 project clear with assigned deliverable owners?

227. How far down?

228. Where does it take place?

229. How much detail?

230. How big is a work-package?

231. What is the probability of completing the ISO 31000 project in less that xx days?

232. When would you develop a Work Breakdown Structure?

233. Why is it useful?

234. Who has to do it?

235. What has to be done?

2.9 WBS Dictionary: ISO 31000

236. Does the contractors system provide unit or lot costs when applicable?

237. The anticipated business volume?

238. Does the contractors system provide for accurate cost accumulation and assignment to control accounts in a manner consistent with the budgets using recognized acceptable costing techniques?

239. Software specification, development, integration, and testing, licenses ?

240. Are the wbs and organizational levels for application of the ISO 31000 projected overhead costs identified?

241. Are data elements reconcilable between internal summary reports and reports forwarded to us?

242. Are overhead cost budgets (or ISO 31000 projections) established on a facility-wide basis at least annually for the life of the contract?

243. Knowledgeable ISO 31000 projections of future performance?

244. Are management actions taken to reduce indirect costs when there are significant adverse variances?

245. Is cost performance measurement at the point

in time most suitable for the category of material involved, and no earlier than the time of actual receipt of material?

246. Where learning is used in developing underlying budgets is there a direct relationship between anticipated learning and time phased budgets?

247. Is undistributed budget limited to contract effort which cannot yet be planned to CWBS elements at or below the level specified for reporting to the Government?

248. Does the contractor use objective results, design reviews and tests to trace schedule performance?

249. Does the contractors system include procedures for measuring the performance of critical subcontractors?

250. Does the cost accumulation system provide for summarization of indirect costs from the point of allocation to the contract total?

251. How many levels?

252. Are procedures established to prevent changes to the contract budget base other than the already stated authorized by contractual action?

253. Performance to date and material commitment?

254. Is authorization of budgets in excess of the contract budget base controlled formally and done with the full knowledge and recognition of the procuring activity?

255. Are current budgets resulting from changes to the authorized work and/or internal replanning, reconcilable to original budgets for specified reporting items?

2.10 Schedule Management Plan: ISO 31000

256. Has a sponsor been identified?

257. Are staff skills known and available for each task?

258. Do all stakeholders know how to access this repository and where to find the ISO 31000 project documentation?

259. Were ISO 31000 project team members involved in detailed estimating and scheduling?

260. Have external dependencies been captured in the schedule?

261. Are the processes for status updates and maintenance defined?

262. Has the business need been clearly defined?

263. Are actuals compared against estimates to analyze and correct variances?

264. Are the processes for schedule assessment and analysis defined?

265. Is the correct WBS element identified for each task and milestone in the IMS?

266. Is the plan consistent with industry best practices?

267. Are changes in deliverable commitments agreed to by all affected groups & individuals?

268. Has the ims content been baselined and is it adequately controlled?

269. Does the ISO 31000 project have a formal ISO 31000 project Charter?

270. Have the key functions and capabilities been defined and assigned to each release or iteration?

271. Have all involved ISO 31000 project stakeholders and work groups committed to the ISO 31000 project?

272. Is documentation created for communication with the suppliers and Vendors?

273. Is pert / critical path or equivalent methodology being used?

274. Is a payment system in place with proper reviews and approvals?

275. Are all attributes of the activities defined, including risk and uncertainty?

2.11 Activity List: ISO 31000

276. How detailed should a ISO 31000 project get?

277. What is the total time required to complete the ISO 31000 project if no delays occur?

278. How do you determine the late start (LS) for each activity?

279. How difficult will it be to do specific activities on this ISO 31000 project?

280. Is there anything planned that does not need to be here?

281. What is the LF and LS for each activity?

282. What went well?

283. What are the critical bottleneck activities?

284. The wbs is developed as part of a joint planning session. and how do you know that youhave done this right?

285. How can the ISO 31000 project be displayed graphically to better visualize the activities?

286. Where will it be performed?

287. For other activities, how much delay can be tolerated?

288. Who will perform the work?

289. What is your organizations history in doing similar activities?

290. In what sequence?

291. When will the work be performed?

292. Can you determine the activity that must finish, before this activity can start?

2.12 Activity Attributes: ISO 31000

293. Has management defined a definite timeframe for the turnaround or ISO 31000 project window?

294. How many days do you need to complete the work scope with a limit of X number of resources?

295. Activity: fair or not fair?

296. How much activity detail is required?

297. Does your organization of the data change its meaning?

298. Where else does it apply?

299. Time for overtime?

300. Can you re-assign any activities to another resource to resolve an over-allocation?

301. Do you feel very comfortable with your prediction?

302. Activity: what is Missing?

303. Can more resources be added?

304. Would you consider either of corresponding activities an outlier?

305. Were there other ways you could have organized the data to achieve similar results?

306. Resource is assigned to?

307. Are the required resources available or need to be acquired?

308. What activity do you think you should spend the most time on?

309. Which method produces the more accurate cost assignment?

310. Have you identified the Activity Leveling Priority code value on each activity?

2.13 Milestone List: ISO 31000

311. Loss of key staff?

312. Calculate how long can activity be delayed?

313. How soon can the activity start?

314. What are your competitors vulnerabilities?

315. Sustaining internal capabilities?

316. Do you foresee any technical risks or developmental challenges?

317. Reliability of data, plan predictability?

318. Usps (unique selling points)?

319. New USPs?

320. Vital contracts and partners?

321. How will the milestone be verified?

322. How late can the activity finish?

323. What has been done so far?

324. How will you get the word out to customers?

325. What specific improvements did you make to the ISO 31000 project proposal since the previous time?

326. Level of the Innovation?

327. How late can each activity be finished and started?

328. Describe your organizations strengths and core competencies. What factors will make your organization succeed?

329. What background experience, skills, and strengths does the team bring to your organization?

330. Describe the concept of the technology, product or service that will be or has been developed. How will it be used?

2.14 Network Diagram: ISO 31000

331. What activities must follow this activity?

332. What are the Key Success Factors?

333. Can you calculate the confidence level?

334. What job or jobs could run concurrently?

335. If a current contract exists, can you provide the vendor name, contract start, and contract expiration date?

336. What is the probability of completing the ISO 31000 project in less that xx days?

337. Where do you schedule uncertainty time?

338. What controls the start and finish of a job?

339. What are the tools?

340. Where do schedules come from?

341. What is the lowest cost to complete this ISO 31000 project in xx weeks?

342. What must be completed before an activity can be started?

343. Are the required resources available?

344. What can be done concurrently?

345. What job or jobs follow it?

346. How confident can you be in your milestone dates and the delivery date?

347. What job or jobs precede it?

348. Which type of network diagram allows you to depict four types of dependencies?

349. Review the logical flow of the network diagram. Take a look at which activities you have first and then sequence the activities. Do they make sense?

350. What to do and When?

2.15 Activity Resource Requirements: ISO 31000

351. Organizational Applicability?

352. How do you handle petty cash?

353. Are there unresolved issues that need to be addressed?

354. Anything else?

355. How do you manage time?

356. Which logical relationship does the PDM use most often?

357. Do you use tools like decomposition and rolling-wave planning to produce the activity list and other outputs?

358. How many signatures do you require on a check and does this match what is in your policy and procedures?

359. Why do you do that?

360. What is the Work Plan Standard?

361. What are constraints that you might find during the Human Resource Planning process?

362. When does monitoring begin?

363. Other support in specific areas?

2.16 Resource Breakdown Structure: ISO 31000

364. How should the information be delivered?

365. Who needs what information?

366. What is ISO 31000 project communication management?

367. What is the purpose of assigning and documenting responsibility?

368. Is predictive resource analysis being done?

369. What is the primary purpose of the human resource plan?

370. Goals for the ISO 31000 project. What is each stakeholders desired outcome for the ISO 31000 project?

371. Any changes from stakeholders?

372. Who delivers the information?

373. What defines a successful ISO 31000 project?

374. Which resources should be in the resource pool?

375. Why do you do it?

376. What is each stakeholders desired outcome for

the ISO 31000 project?

377. Which resource planning tool provides information on resource responsibility and accountability?

378. How can this help you with team building?

379. The list could probably go on, but, the thing that you would most like to know is, How long & How much?

380. What is the difference between % Complete and % work?

2.17 Activity Duration Estimates: ISO 31000

381. Describe a ISO 31000 project that suffered from scope creep. Could it have been avoided?

382. Are many products available?

383. Are procedures defined for calculating cost estimates?

384. What functions does this software provide that cannot be done easily using other tools such as a spreadsheet or database?

385. What are two suggestions for ensuring adequate change control on ISO 31000 projects that involve outside contracts?

386. How difficult will it be to complete specific activities on this ISO 31000 project?

387. What type of activity sequencing method is required for corresponding activities?

388. Does the software appear easy to learn?

389. Which type of mathematical analysis is being used?

390. What tasks must follow this task?

391. Is the cost performance monitored to identify

variances from the plan?

392. Account for the four frames of organizations. How can they help ISO 31000 project managers understand your organizational context for ISO 31000 projects?

393. Are actual ISO 31000 project results compared with planned or expected results to determine the variance?

394. Consider the examples of poor quality in information technology ISO 31000 projects presented in the What Went Wrong?

395. Are risks monitored to determine if an event has occurred or if the mitigation was successful?

396. How difficult will it be to do specific activities on this ISO 31000 project?

397. Do procedures exist that identify when and how human resources are introduced and removed from the ISO 31000 project?

398. How many different communications channels does a ISO 31000 project team with six people have?

399. Do procedures exist describing how the ISO 31000 project scope will be managed?

2.18 Duration Estimating Worksheet: ISO 31000

400. How can the ISO 31000 project be displayed graphically to better visualize the activities?

401. Is a construction detail attached (to aid in explanation)?

402. Science = process: remember the scientific method?

403. What work will be included in the ISO 31000 project?

404. Small or large ISO 31000 project?

405. What questions do you have?

406. What is next?

407. What is your role?

408. Value pocket identification & quantification what are value pockets?

409. What is the total time required to complete the ISO 31000 project if no delays occur?

410. How should ongoing costs be monitored to try to keep the ISO 31000 project within budget?

411. When does your organization expect to be able

to complete it?

412. Does the ISO 31000 project provide innovative ways for stakeholders to overcome obstacles or deliver better outcomes?

413. Define the work as completely as possible. What work will be included in the ISO 31000 project?

414. What is an Average ISO 31000 project?

415. Is the ISO 31000 project responsive to community need?

416. Why estimate costs?

417. Why estimate time and cost?

2.19 Project Schedule: ISO 31000

418. Have all ISO 31000 project delays been adequately accounted for, communicated to all stakeholders and adjustments made in overall ISO 31000 project schedule?

419. How can you fix it?

420. Is ISO 31000 project work proceeding in accordance with the original ISO 31000 project schedule?

421. Why do you think schedule issues often cause the most conflicts on ISO 31000 projects?

422. What does that mean?

423. Is the structure for tracking the ISO 31000 project schedule well defined and assigned to a specific individual?

424. Is infrastructure setup part of your ISO 31000 project?

425. If you can not fix it, how do you do it differently?

426. Are procedures defined by which the ISO 31000 project schedule may be changed?

427. How do you use schedules?

428. Are quality inspections and review activities listed in the ISO 31000 project schedule(s)?

429. Why is software ISO 31000 project disaster so common?

430. How can you minimize or control changes to ISO 31000 project schedules?

431. Month ISO 31000 project take?

432. Your best shot for providing estimations how complex/how much work does the activity require?

433. What is ISO 31000 project management?

434. What is the difference?

2.20 Cost Management Plan: ISO 31000

435. Have all involved ISO 31000 project stakeholders and work groups committed to the ISO 31000 project?

436. Published materials?

437. Vac -variance at completion, how much over/ under budget do you expect to be?

438. Are risk triggers captured?

439. Are estimating assumptions and constraints captured?

440. Are target dates established for each milestone deliverable?

441. Are key risk mitigation strategies added to the ISO 31000 project schedule?

442. Has a structured approach been used to break work effort into manageable components (WBS)?

443. What are the nine areas of expertise?

444. Have all unresolved risks been documented?

445. What would the life cycle costs be?

446. Has a provision been made to reassess ISO 31000 project risks at various ISO 31000 project stages?

447. Is there a requirements change management processes in place?

448. Are trade-offs between accepting the risk and mitigating the risk identified?

449. Will the forecasts be based on trend analysis and earned value statistics?

450. Schedule variances – how will schedule variances be identified and corrected?

451. Are internal ISO 31000 project status meetings held at reasonable intervals?

452. Change types and category – What are the types of changes and what are the techniques to report and control changes?

453. Are all key components of a Quality Assurance Plan present?

2.21 Activity Cost Estimates: ISO 31000

454. How do you change activities?

455. What is your organizations history in doing similar tasks?

456. What is the activity recast of the budget?

457. Certification of actual expenditures?

458. Are data needed on characteristics of care?

459. In which phase of the acquisition process cycle does source qualifications reside?

460. Did the ISO 31000 project team have the right skills?

461. What procedures are put in place regarding bidding and cost comparisons, if any?

462. Were the tasks or work products prepared by the consultant useful?

463. Was the consultant knowledgeable about the program?

464. Review – what are some common errors in activities to avoid?

465. What were things that you need to improve?

466. When do you enter into PPM?

467. Padding is bad and contingencies are good. what is the difference?

468. Were the costs or charges reasonable?

469. How quickly can the task be done with the skills available?

470. How do you fund change orders?

2.22 Cost Estimating Worksheet: ISO 31000

471. What is the estimated labor cost today based upon this information?

472. What can be included?

473. Who is best positioned to know and assist in identifying corresponding factors?

474. What costs are to be estimated?

475. What additional ISO 31000 project(s) could be initiated as a result of this ISO 31000 project?

476. Is the ISO 31000 project responsive to community need?

477. Can a trend be established from historical performance data on the selected measure and are the criteria for using trend analysis or forecasting methods met?

478. What is the purpose of estimating?

479. Will the ISO 31000 project collaborate with the local community and leverage resources?

480. What will others want?

481. Ask: are others positioned to know, are others credible, and will others cooperate?

482. Identify the timeframe necessary to monitor progress and collect data to determine how the selected measure has changed?

483. What happens to any remaining funds not used?

484. Is it feasible to establish a control group arrangement?

485. How will the results be shared and to whom?

486. What info is needed?

487. Does the ISO 31000 project provide innovative ways for stakeholders to overcome obstacles or deliver better outcomes?

2.23 Cost Baseline: ISO 31000

488. Does the suggested change request represent a desired enhancement to the products functionality?

489. Has the actual cost of the ISO 31000 project (or ISO 31000 project phase) been tallied and compared to the approved budget?

490. Is there anything unique in this ISO 31000 projects scope statement that will affect resources?

491. What deliverables come first?

492. Where do changes come from?

493. Has the appropriate access to relevant data and analysis capability been granted?

494. Review your risk triggers -have your risks changed?

495. On budget?

496. Is there anything you need from upper management in order to be successful?

497. Are you asking management for something as a result of this update?

498. How long are you willing to wait before you find out were late?

499. How will cost estimates be used?

500. Will the ISO 31000 project fail if the change request is not executed?

501. How likely is it to go wrong?

502. What threats might prevent you from getting there?

503. Have all approved changes to the schedule baseline been identified and impact on the ISO 31000 project documented?

504. On time?

505. Has the documentation relating to operation and maintenance of the product(s) or service(s) been delivered to, and accepted by, operations management?

506. At which frequency ?

507. Is the requested change request a result of changes in other ISO 31000 project(s)?

2.24 Quality Management Plan: ISO 31000

508. What would be the next steps or what else should you do at this point?

509. Who is responsible for approving the qapp?

510. Are there procedures in place to effectively manage interdependencies with other ISO 31000 projects / systems?

511. Sampling part of task?

512. Who is responsible?

513. What is the return on investment?

514. Are requirements management tracking tools and procedures in place?

515. What is your organizations strategic planning process?

516. Does the program use other agents to collect samples?

517. If it is out of compliance, should the process be amended or should the Plan be amended?

518. How long do you retain data?

519. Are qmps good forever?

520. Who gets results of work?

521. Do trained quality assurance auditors conduct the audits as defined in the Quality Management Plan and scheduled by the ISO 31000 project manager?

522. What are your organizations key processes (product, service, business, and support)?

523. Are there unnecessary steps that are creating bottlenecks and/or causing people to wait?

524. How are calibration records kept?

525. How does your organization ensure the quality, reliability, and user-friendliness of its hardware and software?

526. How do you ensure that protocols are up to date?

2.25 Quality Metrics: ISO 31000

527. What forces exist that would cause them to change?

528. There are many reasons to shore up quality-related metrics, and what metrics are important?

529. Is material complete (and does it meet the standards)?

530. Should a modifier be included?

531. What level of statistical confidence do you use?

532. How is it being measured?

533. Are documents on hand to provide explanations of privacy and confidentiality?

534. Do the operators focus on determining; is there anything you need to worry about?

535. Is quality culture a competitive advantage?

536. Where did complaints, returns and warranty claims come from?

537. Were number of defects identified?

538. Are quality metrics defined?

539. Was review conducted per standard protocols?

540. The metrics–what is being considered?

541. Where is quality now?

542. Subjective quality component: customer satisfaction, how do you measure it?

543. What percentage are outcome-based?

544. Which are the right metrics to use?

545. Filter visualizations of interest?

2.26 Process Improvement Plan: ISO 31000

546. Has the time line required to move measurement results from the points of collection to databases or users been established?

547. Are you making progress on the improvement framework?

548. What personnel are the champions for the initiative?

549. Are you meeting the quality standards?

550. Does your process ensure quality?

551. Purpose of goal: the motive is determined by asking, why do you want to achieve this goal?

552. Have the supporting tools been developed or acquired?

553. What makes people good SPI coaches?

554. Are there forms and procedures to collect and record the data?

555. Are you making progress on the goals?

556. Are you making progress on your improvement plan?

557. Who should prepare the process improvement action plan?

558. Have the frequency of collection and the points in the process where measurements will be made been determined?

559. What personnel are the sponsors for that initiative?

560. How do you manage quality?

561. What personnel are the coaches for your initiative?

562. Why quality management?

563. Where do you want to be?

2.27 Responsibility Assignment Matrix: ISO 31000

564. Do you need to convince people that its well worth the time and effort?

565. Undistributed budgets, if any?

566. Identify and isolate causes of favorable and unfavorable cost and schedule variances?

567. What can you do to improve productivity?

568. The already stated responsible for overhead performance control of related costs?

569. The total budget for the contract (including estimates for authorized and unpriced work)?

570. What tool can show you individual and group allocations?

571. Do all the identified groups or people really need to be consulted?

572. How cost benefit analysis?

573. Evaluate the performance of operating organizations?

574. Do others have the time to dedicate to your ISO 31000 project?

575. What do you do when people do not respond?

576. Most people let you know when others re too busy, and are others really too busy?

577. Is it safe to say you can handle more work or that some tasks you are supposed to do arent worth doing?

578. Budgets assigned to major functional organizations?

579. What does wbs accomplish?

580. The staff interests – is the group or the person interested in working for this ISO 31000 project?

581. Does each role with Accountable responsibility have the authority within your organization to make the required decisions?

582. Budgeted cost for work performed?

2.28 Roles and Responsibilities: ISO 31000

583. Is feedback clearly communicated and non-judgmental?

584. Do the values and practices inherent in the culture of your organization foster or hinder the process?

585. Is there a training program in place for stakeholders covering expectations, roles and responsibilities and any addition knowledge others need to be good stakeholders?

586. Does the team have access to and ability to use data analysis tools?

587. What expectations were met?

588. Are ISO 31000 project team roles and responsibilities identified and documented?

589. Influence: what areas of organizational decision making are you able to influence when you do not have authority to make the final decision?

590. Does your vision/mission support a culture of quality data?

591. Are your policies supportive of a culture of quality data?

592. What specific behaviors did you observe?

593. Implementation of actions: Who are the responsible units?

594. What should you do now to ensure that you are meeting all expectations of your current position?

595. What is working well?

596. Key conclusions and recommendations: Are conclusions and recommendations relevant and acceptable?

597. Have you ever been a part of this team?

598. What is working well within your organizations performance management system?

599. Was the expectation clearly communicated?

600. Are your budgets supportive of a culture of quality data?

2.29 Human Resource Management Plan: ISO 31000

601. Does the schedule include ISO 31000 project management time and change request analysis time?

602. What skills, knowledge and experiences are required?

603. Does the ISO 31000 project have a Statement of Work?

604. Are tasks tracked by hours?

605. Has the schedule been baselined?

606. Is quality monitored from the perspective of the customers needs and expectations?

607. Quality assurance overheads?

608. Are software metrics formally captured, analyzed and used as a basis for other ISO 31000 project estimates?

609. How will the ISO 31000 project manage expectations & meet needs and requirements?

610. Is a pmo (ISO 31000 project management office) in place and provide oversight to the ISO 31000 project?

611. Has a capability assessment been conducted?

612. Do all stakeholders know how to access this repository and where to find the ISO 31000 project documentation?

613. Are the right people being attracted and retained to meet the future challenges?

614. What were things that you did well, and could improve, and how?

615. Is current scope of the ISO 31000 project substantially different than that originally defined?

616. Are quality inspections and review activities listed in the ISO 31000 project schedule(s)?

2.30 Communications Management Plan: ISO 31000

617. Are stakeholders internal or external?

618. Do you ask; can you recommend others for you to talk with about this initiative?

619. Who are the members of the governing body?

620. Will messages be directly related to the release strategy or phases of the ISO 31000 project?

621. Do you then often overlook a key stakeholder or stakeholder group?

622. What help do you and your team need from the stakeholder?

623. Who will use or be affected by the result of a ISO 31000 project?

624. Who to learn from?

625. How were corresponding initiatives successful?

626. How do you manage communications?

627. Who did you turn to if you had questions?

628. Where do team members get information?

629. What is the political influence?

630. What is ISO 31000 project communications management?

631. Do you have members of your team responsible for certain stakeholders?

632. Timing: when do the effects of the communication take place?

633. Which stakeholders can influence others?

634. How did the term stakeholder originate?

2.31 Risk Management Plan: ISO 31000

635. Does the customer have a solid idea of what is required?

636. Financial risk: can your organization afford to undertake the ISO 31000 project?

637. For software; does the software interface with new or unproven hardware or unproven vendor products?

638. Should the risk be taken at all?

639. Prioritized components/features?

640. Can you stabilize dynamic risk factors?

641. Are team members trained in the use of the tools?

642. Risk may be made during which step of risk management?

643. Do the people have the right combinations of skills?

644. How do you manage ISO 31000 project Risk?

645. Market risk -will the new service or product be useful to your organization or marketable to others?

646. Are enough people available?

647. Are the metrics meaningful and useful?

648. Are formal technical reviews part of this process?

649. Does the customer understand the software process?

650. How much risk protection can you afford?

651. Was an original risk assessment/risk management plan completed?

652. How quickly does this item need to be resolved?

2.32 Risk Register: ISO 31000

653. User involvement: do you have the right users?

654. Why would you develop a risk register?

655. What is the reason for current performance gaps and do the risks and opportunities identified previously account for this?

656. When would you develop a risk register?

657. What risks might negatively or positively affect achieving the ISO 31000 project objectives?

658. Risk categories: what are the main categories of risks that should be addressed on this ISO 31000 project?

659. How often will the Risk Management Plan and Risk Register be formally reviewed, and by whom?

660. What is the probability and impact of the risk occurring?

661. What are your key risks/show istoppers and what is being done to manage them?

662. Does the evidence highlight any areas to advance opportunities or foster good relations. If yes what steps will be taken?

663. Risk probability and impact: how will the probabilities and impacts of risk items be assessed?

664. What would the impact to the ISO 31000 project objectives be should the risk arise?

665. Are there other alternative controls that could be implemented?

666. What should the audit role be in establishing a risk management process?

667. Are your objectives at risk?

668. What are the main aims, objectives of the policy, strategy, or service and the intended outcomes?

669. Cost/benefit – how much will the proposed mitigations cost and how does this cost compare with the potential cost of the risk event/situation should it occur?

670. What should you do when?

671. Preventative actions - planned actions to reduce the likelihood a risk will occur and/or reduce the seriousness should it occur. What should you do now?

672. Are implemented controls working as others should?

2.33 Probability and Impact Assessment: ISO 31000

673. What are the likely future requirements?

674. How would you suggest monitoring for risk transition indicators?

675. Do you manage the process through use of metrics?

676. Who are the international/overseas ISO 31000 project partners (equipment supplier/supplier/consultant/contractor) for this ISO 31000 project?

677. How will economic events and trends likely affect the ISO 31000 project?

678. Is the customer technically sophisticated in the product area?

679. Will there be an increase in the political conservatism?

680. What significant shift will occur in governmental policies, laws, and regulations pertaining to specific industries?

681. How risk averse are you?

682. Which of your ISO 31000 projects should be selected when compared with other ISO 31000 projects?

683. Risks should be identified during which phase of ISO 31000 project management life cycle?

684. What are the risks involved in appointing external agencies to manage the ISO 31000 project?

685. Which of corresponding risk factors can be avoided altogether?

686. What should be done with non-critical risks?

687. Management -what contingency plans do you have if the risk becomes a reality?

688. Have top software and customer managers formally committed to support the ISO 31000 project?

689. My ISO 31000 project leader has suddenly left your organization, what do you do?

690. Are people attending meetings and doing work?

691. Are ISO 31000 project requirements stable?

692. What is the experience (performance, attitude, business ethics, etc.) in the past with contractors?

2.34 Probability and Impact Matrix: ISO 31000

693. How are the local factors going to affect the absorption?

694. What are the chances the risk events will occur?

695. What do you expect?

696. Is a software ISO 31000 project management tool available?

697. Economic to take on the ISO 31000 project?

698. What things are likely to change?

699. Is the ISO 31000 project cutting across the entire organization?

700. What can go wrong?

701. Which role do you have in the ISO 31000 project?

702. Is the process supported by tools?

703. Which is the BEST thing to do?

704. What is the industrial relations prevailing in this organization?

705. What is the risk appetite?

706. What will be the likely political environment during the life of the ISO 31000 project?

707. How can you understand and diagnose risks and identify sources?

708. What needs to be DONE?

709. Who is going to be the consortium leader?

710. What can possibly go wrong?

2.35 Risk Data Sheet: ISO 31000

711. What are you here for (Mission)?

712. Risk of what?

713. Are new hazards created?

714. Has the most cost-effective solution been chosen?

715. Who has a vested interest in how you perform as your organization (our stakeholders)?

716. What do you know?

717. What was measured?

718. How do you handle product safely?

719. Potential for recurrence?

720. If it happens, what are the consequences?

721. What can happen?

722. What were the Causes that contributed?

723. Whom do you serve (customers)?

724. How can it happen?

725. What is the chance that it will happen?

726. What can you do?

727. What do people affected think about the need for, and practicality of preventive measures?

728. How reliable is the data source?

2.36 Procurement Management Plan: ISO 31000

729. Are enough systems & user personnel assigned to the ISO 31000 project?

730. Are change requests logged and managed?

731. Are action items captured and managed?

732. Is there a formal set of procedures supporting Issues Management?

733. Is there an issues management plan in place?

734. How and when do you enter into ISO 31000 project Procurement Management?

735. Specific - is the objective clear in terms of what, how, when, and where the situation will be changed?

736. Are the ISO 31000 project plans updated on a frequent basis?

737. Is the ISO 31000 project schedule available for all ISO 31000 project team members to review?

738. Have all documents been archived in a ISO 31000 project repository for each release?

739. Public engagement – did you get it right?

740. Has the budget been baselined?

741. Are ISO 31000 project team members committed fulltime?

742. Does the schedule include ISO 31000 project management time and change request analysis time?

743. What are things that you need to improve?

2.37 Source Selection Criteria: ISO 31000

744. What source selection software is your team using?

745. Is there collaboration among your evaluators?

746. What are the guidelines regarding award without considerations?

747. Do you want to have them collaborate at subfactor level?

748. Can you identify proposed teaming partners and/or subcontractors and consider the nature and extent of proposed involvement in satisfying the ISO 31000 project requirements?

749. Are resultant proposal revisions allowed?

750. Does the evaluation of any change include an impact analysis; how will the change affect the scope, time, cost, and quality of the goods or services being provided?

751. Is a cost realism analysis used?

752. What are the limitations on pre-competitive range communications?

753. What are the most common types of rating systems?

754. In the technical/management area, what criteria do you use to determine the final evaluation ratings?

755. What should a Draft Request for Proposal (DRFP) include?

756. What documentation is needed for a tradeoff decision?

757. Which contract type places the most risk on the seller?

758. What should preproposal conferences accomplish?

759. When and what information can be considered with offerors regarding past performance?

760. Who must be notified?

761. Are they compliant with all technical requirements?

762. Are responses to considerations adequate?

763. What is price analysis and when should it be performed?

2.38 Stakeholder Management Plan: ISO 31000

764. Does the ISO 31000 project have a formal ISO 31000 project Charter?

765. Are communication systems proposed compatible with staff skills and experience?

766. Who is responsible for arranging and managing the review(s)?

767. Are post milestone ISO 31000 project reviews (PMPR) conducted with your organization at least once a year?

768. Are regulatory inspections considered part of quality control?

769. Have adequate resources been provided by management to ensure ISO 31000 project success?

770. Is staff trained on the software technologies that are being used on the ISO 31000 project?

771. Have reserves been created to address risks?

772. Is there a Steering Committee in place?

773. What is meant by managing the triple constraint?

774. Are the schedule estimates reasonable given the ISO 31000 project?

775. Why would you develop a ISO 31000 project Execution Plan?

776. Have activity relationships and interdependencies within tasks been adequately identified?

777. What guidelines or procedures currently exist that must be adhered to (eg departmental accounting procedures)?

778. Were ISO 31000 project team members involved in detailed estimating and scheduling?

779. Have all team members been part of identifying risks?

780. What are the advantages and disadvantages of using external contracted resources?

2.39 Change Management Plan: ISO 31000

781. Does this change represent a completely new process for your organization, or a different application of an existing process?

782. Will all field readiness criteria have been practically met prior to training roll-out?

783. What risks may occur upfront, during implementation and after implementation?

784. What are the dependencies?

785. What can you do to minimise misinterpretation and negative perceptions?

786. What is the reason for the communication?

787. Has the training provider been established?

788. Who will be the change levers?

789. What did the people around you say about it?

790. Who might be able to help you the most?

791. What are the specific target groups/audiences that will be impacted by this change?

792. When does it make sense to customize?

793. What risks may occur upfront?

794. Do you need a new organization structure?

795. Has the target training audience been identified and nominated?

796. What are the major changes to processes?

797. How badly can information be misinterpreted?

798. What are the specific target groups / audience that will be impacted by this change?

3.0 Executing Process Group: ISO 31000

799. Are the necessary foundations in place to ensure the sustainability of the results of the programme?

800. What are the critical steps involved with strategy mapping?

801. When do you share the scorecard with managers?

802. Measurable - are the targets measurable?

803. How does a ISO 31000 project life cycle differ from a product life cycle?

804. Are escalated issues resolved promptly?

805. What is the shortest possible time it will take to complete this ISO 31000 project?

806. What are the ISO 31000 project management deliverables of each process group?

807. Does software appear easy to learn?

808. Just how important is your work to the overall success of the ISO 31000 project?

809. If action is called for, what form should it take?

810. How will you know you did it?

811. Do the partners have sufficient financial capacity to keep up the benefits produced by the programme?

812. What is the difference between using brainstorming and the Delphi technique for risk identification?

813. What are the critical steps involved in selecting measures and initiatives?

814. How does ISO 31000 project management relate to other disciplines?

815. What is the critical path for this ISO 31000 project and how long is it?

816. How well did the chosen processes fit the needs of the ISO 31000 project?

3.1 Team Member Status Report: ISO 31000

817. What specific interest groups do you have in place?

818. Does every department have to have a ISO 31000 project Manager on staff?

819. Do you have an Enterprise ISO 31000 project Management Office (EPMO)?

820. Will the staff do training or is that done by a third party?

821. How does this product, good, or service meet the needs of the ISO 31000 project and your organization as a whole?

822. The problem with Reward & Recognition Programs is that the truly deserving people all too often get left out. How can you make it practical?

823. What is to be done?

824. Is there evidence that staff is taking a more professional approach toward management of your organizations ISO 31000 projects?

825. How can you make it practical?

826. Are your organizations ISO 31000 projects more successful over time?

827. Does the product, good, or service already exist within your organization?

828. Does your organization have the means (staff, money, contract, etc.) to produce or to acquire the product, good, or service?

829. How it is to be done?

830. Why is it to be done?

831. How much risk is involved?

832. When a teams productivity and success depend on collaboration and the efficient flow of information, what generally fails them?

833. Are the attitudes of staff regarding ISO 31000 project work improving?

834. How will resource planning be done?

835. Are the products of your organizations ISO 31000 projects meeting customers objectives?

3.2 Change Request: ISO 31000

836. What kind of information about the change request needs to be captured?

837. Customer acceptance plan how will the customer verify the change has been implemented successfully?

838. Have scm procedures for noting the change, recording it, and reporting it been followed?

839. Will this change conflict with other requirements changes (e.g., lead to conflicting operational scenarios)?

840. Are you implementing itil processes?

841. What are the requirements for urgent changes?

842. When do you create a change request?

843. What are the duties of the change control team?

844. Are there requirements attributes that are strongly related to the complexity and size?

845. Will there be a change request form in use?

846. How is quality being addressed on the ISO 31000 project?

847. How can you ensure that changes have been made properly?

848. For which areas does this operating procedure apply?

849. Should a more thorough impact analysis be conducted?

850. How do you get changes (code) out in a timely manner?

851. When to submit a change request?

852. Should staff call into the helpdesk or go to the website?

853. How well do experienced software developers predict software change?

854. Why do you want to have a change control system?

3.3 Change Log: ISO 31000

855. How does this relate to the standards developed for specific business processes?

856. Is the change request within ISO 31000 project scope?

857. Is this a mandatory replacement?

858. Who initiated the change request?

859. When was the request approved?

860. Is the requested change request a result of changes in other ISO 31000 project(s)?

861. When was the request submitted?

862. How does this change affect the timeline of the schedule?

863. Will the ISO 31000 project fail if the change request is not executed?

864. Is the change backward compatible without limitations?

865. Does the suggested change request seem to represent a necessary enhancement to the product?

866. Do the described changes impact on the integrity or security of the system?

867. Is the submitted change a new change or a modification of a previously approved change?

868. How does this change affect scope?

869. Is the change request open, closed or pending?

3.4 Decision Log: ISO 31000

870. At what point in time does loss become unacceptable?

871. What eDiscovery problem or issue did your organization set out to fix or make better?

872. What alternatives/risks were considered?

873. Behaviors; what are guidelines that the team has identified that will assist them with getting the most out of team meetings?

874. Meeting purpose; why does this team meet?

875. Is everything working as expected?

876. What is the average size of your matters in an applicable measurement?

877. Linked to original objective?

878. What is your overall strategy for quality control / quality assurance procedures?

879. Which variables make a critical difference?

880. How effective is maintaining the log at facilitating organizational learning?

881. Does anything need to be adjusted?

882. What was the rationale for the decision?

883. Adversarial environment. is your opponent open to a non-traditional workflow, or will it likely challenge anything you do?

884. Who will be given a copy of this document and where will it be kept?

885. How does an increasing emphasis on cost containment influence the strategies and tactics used?

886. Who is the decisionmaker?

887. How does the use a Decision Support System influence the strategies/tactics or costs?

888. Is your opponent open to a non-traditional workflow, or will it likely challenge anything you do?

889. How consolidated and comprehensive a story can you tell by capturing currently available incident data in a central location and through a log of key decisions during an incident?

3.5 Quality Audit: ISO 31000

890. Are measuring and test equipment that have been placed out of service suitably identified and excluded from use in any device reconditioning operation?

891. How does the organization know that its industry and community engagement planning and management systems are appropriately effective and constructive in enabling relationships with key stakeholder groups?

892. How does your organization know that its general support services planning and management systems are appropriately effective and constructive?

893. How are you auditing your organizations compliance with regulations?

894. Are there appropriate indicators for monitoring the effectiveness and efficiency of processes?

895. How does your organization ensure that equipment is appropriately maintained and producing valid results?

896. Are multiple statements on the same issue consistent with each other?

897. How does your organization know that it is appropriately effective and constructive in preparing its staff for organizational aspirations?

898. What review processes are in place for your organizations major activities?

899. Is the process of self review, learning and improvement endemic throughout your organization?

900. Is progress against the intentions measurable?

901. How does your organization know that its system for examining work done is appropriately effective and constructive?

902. Are goals well supported with strategies, operational plans, manuals and training?

903. How does your organization know that its systems for providing high quality consultancy services to external parties are appropriately effective and constructive?

904. How does your organization know that its information technology system is serving its needs as effectively and constructively as is appropriate?

905. How does your organization know that its Governance system is appropriately effective and constructive?

906. Health and safety arrangements; stress management workshops. How does your organization know that it provides a safe and healthy environment?

907. How does your organization know that the support for its staff is appropriately effective and constructive?

908. How does your organization know that its support services planning and management systems are appropriately effective and constructive?

909. What are your supplier audits?

3.6 Team Directory: ISO 31000

910. Does a ISO 31000 project team directory list all resources assigned to the ISO 31000 project?

911. Who will write the meeting minutes and distribute?

912. Process decisions: are there any statutory or regulatory issues relevant to the timely execution of work?

913. Timing: when do the effects of communication take place?

914. Have you decided when to celebrate the ISO 31000 projects completion date?

915. How do unidentified risks impact the outcome of the ISO 31000 project?

916. Process decisions: how well was task order work performed?

917. Decisions: what could be done better to improve the quality of the constructed product?

918. When does information need to be distributed?

919. Contract requirements complied with?

920. How does the team resolve conflicts and ensure tasks are completed?

921. How will the team handle changes?

922. Who are your stakeholders (customers, sponsors, end users, team members)?

923. Who should receive information (all stakeholders)?

924. Where should the information be distributed?

925. What are you going to deliver or accomplish?

926. Is construction on schedule?

927. Process decisions: are all start-up, turn over and close out requirements of the contract satisfied?

928. Who will talk to the customer?

3.7 Team Operating Agreement: ISO 31000

929. Reimbursements: how will the team members be reimbursed for expenses and time commitments?

930. Are there more than two native languages represented by your team?

931. Do you begin with a question to engage everyone?

932. Do you solicit member feedback about meetings and what would make them better?

933. Must your team members rely on the expertise of other members to complete tasks?

934. Do you send out the agenda and meeting materials in advance?

935. Resource allocation: how will individual team members account for time and expenses, and how will this be allocated in the team budget?

936. How do you want to be thought of and known within your organization?

937. What administrative supports will be put in place to support the team and the teams supervisor?

938. Do you leverage technology engagement tools group chat, polls, screen sharing, etc.?

939. What are the boundaries (organizational or geographic) within which you operate?

940. To whom do you deliver your services?

941. Do you vary your voice pace, tone and pitch to engage participants and gain involvement?

942. Do you post meeting notes and the recording (if used) and notify participants?

943. Are there more than two national cultures represented by your team?

944. Do you ensure that all participants know how to use the required technology?

945. Do you prevent individuals from dominating the meeting?

946. Does your team need access to all documents and information at all times?

947. What is the anticipated procedure (recruitment, solicitation of volunteers, or assignment) for selecting team members?

948. Is compensation based on team and individual performance?

3.8 Team Performance Assessment: ISO 31000

949. How do you recognize and praise members for contributions?

950. When a reviewer complains about method variance, what is the essence of the complaint?

951. To what degree do team members agree with the goals, relative importance, and the ways in which achievement will be measured?

952. To what degree are staff involved as partners in the improvement process?

953. To what degree does the teams purpose constitute a broader, deeper aspiration than just accomplishing short-term goals?

954. To what degree will new and supplemental skills be introduced as the need is recognized?

955. To what degree can team members meet frequently enough to accomplish the teams ends?

956. To what degree do team members feel that the purpose of the team is important, if not exciting?

957. To what degree will the team ensure that all members equitably share the work essential to the success of the team?

958. When does the medium matter?

959. To what degree are the relative importance and priority of the goals clear to all team members?

960. To what degree do team members frequently explore the teams purpose and its implications?

961. To what degree can team members vigorously define the teams purpose in considerations with others who are not part of the functioning team?

962. Do you give group members authority to make at least some important decisions?

963. To what degree can all members engage in open and interactive considerations?

964. Can team performance be reliably measured in simulator and live exercises using the same assessment tool?

965. To what degree do members articulate the goals beyond the team membership?

966. What are you doing specifically to develop the leaders around you?

967. To what degree does the teams work approach provide opportunity for members to engage in results-based evaluation?

968. What are teams?

3.9 Team Member Performance Assessment: ISO 31000

969. Are assessment validation activities performed?

970. What variables that affect team members achievement are within your control?

971. Did training work?

972. Is there reluctance to join a team?

973. Are there any safeguards to prevent intentional or unintentional rating errors?

974. What specific plans do you have for developing effective cross-platform assessments in a blended learning environment?

975. In what areas would you like to concentrate your knowledge and resources?

976. To what degree do team members understand one anothers roles and skills?

977. What future plans (e.g., modifications) do you have for your program?

978. To what degree do the goals specify concrete team work products?

979. What tools are available to determine whether all contract functional and compliance areas of

performance objectives, measures, and incentives have been met?

980. Are any validation activities performed?

981. How will you identify your Team Leaders?

982. What is needed for effective data teams?

983. To what degree does the team possess adequate membership to achieve its ends?

984. What is the large, desired outcome?

985. New skills/knowledge gained this year?

986. What instructional strategies were developed/ incorporated (e.g., direct instruction, indirect instruction, experiential learning, independent study, interactive instruction)?

987. What does collaboration look like?

3.10 Issue Log: ISO 31000

988. Who is the issue assigned to?

989. What is the status of the issue?

990. Are they needed?

991. Do you feel more overwhelmed by stakeholders?

992. Why do you manage human resources?

993. Do you prepare stakeholder engagement plans?

994. Why do you manage communications?

995. Which team member will work with each stakeholder?

996. Who is the stakeholder?

997. Are there too many who have an interest in some aspect of your work?

998. Is access to the Issue Log controlled?

999. What is a Stakeholder?

1000. Why not more evaluators?

1001. Is there an important stakeholder who is actively opposed and will not receive messages?

1002. What approaches do you use?

1003. Are you constantly rushing from meeting to meeting?

1004. How were past initiatives successful?

1005. Are there potential barriers between the team and the stakeholder?

1006. What help do you and your team need from the stakeholders?

1007. Are the ISO 31000 project issues uniquely identified, including to which product they refer?

4.0 Monitoring and Controlling Process Group: ISO 31000

1008. Do the products created live up to the necessary quality?

1009. Is there undesirable impact on staff or resources?

1010. How is agile portfolio management done?

1011. Does the solution fit in with organizations technical architectural requirements?

1012. How will staff learn how to use the deliverables?

1013. How to ensure validity, quality and consistency?

1014. Change, where should you look for problems?

1015. Is the verbiage used appropriate and understandable?

1016. How are you doing?

1017. How well did the chosen processes fit the needs of the ISO 31000 project?

1018. Who needs to be engaged upfront to ensure use of results?

1019. When will the ISO 31000 project be done?

1020. How should needs be met?

1021. What good practices or successful experiences or transferable examples have been identified?

1022. Feasibility: how much money, time, and effort can you put into this?

1023. What are the goals of the program?

1024. What is the expected monetary value of the ISO 31000 project?

1025. How many more potential communications channels were introduced by the discovery of the new stakeholders?

4.1 Project Performance Report: ISO 31000

1026. How will procurement be coordinated with other ISO 31000 project aspects, such as scheduling and performance reporting?

1027. To what degree do team members articulate the teams work approach?

1028. What degree are the relative importance and priority of the goals clear to all team members?

1029. To what degree are the demands of the task compatible with and converge with the mission and functions of the formal organization?

1030. To what degree does the teams work approach provide opportunity for members to engage in open interaction?

1031. To what degree are the skill areas critical to team performance present?

1032. To what degree does the teams work approach provide opportunity for members to engage in fact-based problem solving?

1033. To what degree will team members, individually and collectively, commit time to help themselves and others learn and develop skills?

1034. To what degree is there a sense that only the

team can succeed?

1035. To what degree does the formal organization make use of individual resources and meet individual needs?

1036. To what degree are the goals ambitious?

1037. To what degree does the teams purpose contain themes that are particularly meaningful and memorable?

1038. To what degree are the demands of the task compatible with and converge with the relationships of the informal organization?

1039. To what degree do the structures of the formal organization motivate taskrelevant behavior and facilitate task completion?

4.2 Variance Analysis: ISO 31000

1040. Are material costs reported within the same period as that in which BCWP is earned for that material?

1041. Are overhead cost budgets established for each department which has authority to incur overhead costs?

1042. How are variances affected by multiple material and labor categories?

1043. Are all authorized tasks assigned to identified organizational elements?

1044. How does your organization allocate the cost of shared expenses and services?

1045. Is the anticipated (firm and potential) business base ISO 31000 projected in a rational, consistent manner?

1046. How does the monthly budget compare to the actual experience?

1047. What are the actual costs to date?

1048. What can be the cause of an increase in costs?

1049. How are material, labor, and overhead standards set?

1050. Do work packages consist of discrete tasks

which are adequately described?

1051. Are procedures for variance analysis documented and consistently applied at the control account level and selected WBS and organizational levels at least monthly as a routine task?

1052. Are records maintained to show how management reserves are used?

1053. Why do variances exist?

1054. Are the wbs and organizational levels for application of the ISO 31000 projected overhead costs identified?

1055. What are the direct labor dollars and/or hours?

1056. Are the actual costs used for variance analysis reconcilable with data from the accounting system?

1057. Do the rates and prices remain constant throughout the year?

1058. Is the market likely to continue to grow at this rate next year?

1059. What is the total budget for the ISO 31000 project (including estimates for authorized and unpriced work)?

4.3 Earned Value Status: ISO 31000

1060. Verification is a process of ensuring that the developed system satisfies the stakeholders agreements and specifications; Are you building the product right? What do you verify?

1061. How much is it going to cost by the finish?

1062. Earned value can be used in almost any ISO 31000 project situation and in almost any ISO 31000 project environment. it may be used on large ISO 31000 projects, medium sized ISO 31000 projects, tiny ISO 31000 projects (in cut-down form), complex and simple ISO 31000 projects and in any market sector. some people, of course, know all about earned value, they have used it for years - but perhaps not as effectively as they could have?

1063. When is it going to finish?

1064. Validation is a process of ensuring that the developed system will actually achieve the stakeholders desired outcomes; Are you building the right product? What do you validate?

1065. Where are your problem areas?

1066. If earned value management (EVM) is so good in determining the true status of a ISO 31000 project and ISO 31000 project its completion, why is it that hardly any one uses it in information systems related ISO 31000 projects?

1067. How does this compare with other ISO 31000 projects?

1068. What is the unit of forecast value?

1069. Where is evidence-based earned value in your organization reported?

1070. Are you hitting your ISO 31000 projects targets?

4.4 Risk Audit: ISO 31000

1071. Does the customer understand the process?

1072. Is the auditor truly independent?

1073. How will you maximise opportunities?

1074. What events or circumstances could affect the achievement of your objectives?

1075. Have reasonable steps been taken to reduce the risks to acceptable levels?

1076. Are you aware of the industry standards that apply to your operations?

1077. Does the adoption of a business risk audit approach change internal control documentation and testing practices?

1078. What expertise do auditors need to generate effective business-level risk assessments, and to what extent do auditors currently possess the already stated attributes?

1079. What are the legal implications of not identifying a complete universe of business risks?

1080. Is the number of people on the ISO 31000 project team adequate to do the job?

1081. Have top software and customer managers formally committed to support the ISO 31000 project?

1082. Does willful intent modify risk-based auditing?

1083. Does the team have the right mix of skills?

1084. Will safety checks of personal equipment supplied by competitors be conducted?

1085. What is the Board doing to assure measurement and improve outcomes and quality and reduce avoidable adverse events?

1086. Does your organization communicate regularly and effectively with its members?

1087. Do you have an understanding of insurance claims processes?

1088. Do end-users have realistic expectations?

1089. Do you have a consistent repeatable process that is actually used?

1090. Where will the next scandal or adverse media involving your organization come from?

4.5 Contractor Status Report: ISO 31000

1091. What process manages the contracts?

1092. What was the budget or estimated cost for your organizations services?

1093. What was the actual budget or estimated cost for your organizations services?

1094. Describe how often regular updates are made to the proposed solution. Are corresponding regular updates included in the standard maintenance plan?

1095. What are the minimum and optimal bandwidth requirements for the proposed solution?

1096. How does the proposed individual meet each requirement?

1097. How long have you been using the services?

1098. What is the average response time for answering a support call?

1099. What was the overall budget or estimated cost?

1100. What was the final actual cost?

1101. If applicable; describe your standard schedule for new software version releases. Are new software version releases included in the standard maintenance plan?

1102. How is risk transferred?

1103. Who can list a ISO 31000 project as organization experience, your organization or a previous employee of your organization?

1104. Are there contractual transfer concerns?

4.6 Formal Acceptance: ISO 31000

1105. Did the ISO 31000 project achieve its MOV?

1106. Have all comments been addressed?

1107. Does it do what ISO 31000 project team said it would?

1108. Did the ISO 31000 project manager and team act in a professional and ethical manner?

1109. What lessons were learned about your ISO 31000 project management methodology?

1110. Was the ISO 31000 project managed well?

1111. What is the Acceptance Management Process?

1112. General estimate of the costs and times to complete the ISO 31000 project?

1113. Who would use it?

1114. Is formal acceptance of the ISO 31000 project product documented and distributed?

1115. Was the sponsor/customer satisfied?

1116. What can you do better next time?

1117. Do you perform formal acceptance or burn-in tests?

1118. What was done right?

1119. How well did the team follow the methodology?

1120. Was the ISO 31000 project goal achieved?

1121. What features, practices, and processes proved to be strengths or weaknesses?

1122. How does your team plan to obtain formal acceptance on your ISO 31000 project?

1123. What are the requirements against which to test, Who will execute?

1124. Was business value realized?

5.0 Closing Process Group: ISO 31000

1125. What were the desired outcomes?

1126. What is the overall risk of the ISO 31000 project to your organization?

1127. Who are the ISO 31000 project stakeholders?

1128. What can you do better next time, and what specific actions can you take to improve?

1129. How well did you do?

1130. Are there funding or time constraints?

1131. What areas were overlooked on this ISO 31000 project?

1132. Was the user/client satisfied with the end product?

1133. What is the risk of failure to your organization?

1134. What could have been improved?

1135. What do you need to do?

1136. What is an Encumbrance?

1137. How well did the chosen processes fit the needs of the ISO 31000 project?

1138. What is the amount of funding and what ISO

31000 project phases are funded?

5.1 Procurement Audit: ISO 31000

1139. Are approval limits covered in written procedures?

1140. Is the performance of the procurement function/unit regularly evaluated?

1141. Are existing suppliers that have a special right to be consulted being contacted?

1142. Is there any objection?

1143. Were standards, certifications and evidence required admissible?

1144. Where funding is being arranged by borrowings, do corresponding have the necessary approval and legal authority?

1145. Did your organization permit tenderers to submit variants, thus offering space for creative solutions and added value?

1146. Are the right skills, experiences and competencies present in the acquisition workgroup and are the necessary outside specialists involved in part of the process?

1147. Is the functioning of automatic disbursement programs tested by an independent party?

1148. Are petty cash funds operated on an imprest basis?

1149. Are the established budget and timetable (milestones) respected?

1150. Are checks used in numeric sequence?

1151. Does each policy statement contain the legal reference(s) on which the policy is based?

1152. Has the award included no items different from the already stated contained in bid specifications?

1153. Did your organization decide for an appropriate and admissible procurement procedure?

1154. Which contracts have been awarded for works, supply of products or provision of services?

1155. Is the purchase order form clear and complete so that the vendor understands all terms and conditions?

1156. Was invitation to tender to each specific contract issued after the evaluation of the indicative tenders was completed?

1157. Are risks in the external environment identified, for example: Budgetary constraints?

1158. Was the overall procurement done within a reasonable time?

5.2 Contract Close-Out: ISO 31000

1159. Have all contracts been completed?

1160. Parties: who is involved?

1161. Has each contract been audited to verify acceptance and delivery?

1162. Have all contract records been included in the ISO 31000 project archives?

1163. Change in attitude or behavior?

1164. Change in knowledge?

1165. Change in circumstances?

1166. Was the contract type appropriate?

1167. How/when used ?

1168. How does it work?

1169. What is capture management?

1170. How is the contracting office notified of the automatic contract close-out?

1171. Was the contract complete without requiring numerous changes and revisions?

1172. Was the contract sufficiently clear so as not to result in numerous disputes and misunderstandings?

1173. What happens to the recipient of services?

1174. Have all contracts been closed?

1175. Have all acceptance criteria been met prior to final payment to contractors?

1176. Parties: Authorized?

1177. Are the signers the authorized officials?

5.3 Project or Phase Close-Out: ISO 31000

1178. Who controlled the resources for the ISO 31000 project?

1179. Did the ISO 31000 project management methodology work?

1180. Were messages directly related to the release strategy or phases of the ISO 31000 project?

1181. What security considerations needed to be addressed during the procurement life cycle?

1182. What could be done to improve the process?

1183. What is the information level of detail required for each stakeholder?

1184. What hierarchical authority does the stakeholder have in your organization?

1185. Was the schedule met?

1186. What was learned?

1187. What are the marketing communication needs for each stakeholder?

1188. Is the lesson based on actual ISO 31000 project experience rather than on independent research?

1189. If you were the ISO 31000 project sponsor, how would you determine which ISO 31000 project team(s) and/or individuals deserve recognition?

1190. Have business partners been involved extensively, and what data was required for them?

1191. How often did each stakeholder need an update?

1192. Who is responsible for award close-out?

1193. Who controlled key decisions that were made?

1194. Who exerted influence that has positively affected or negatively impacted the ISO 31000 project?

1195. What are the mandatory communication needs for each stakeholder?

5.4 Lessons Learned: ISO 31000

1196. What are the influence patterns?

1197. How long did redeployment take?

1198. How much communication is task-related?

1199. How was the quality of products/processes assured?

1200. What skills are required for the task?

1201. What is your overall assessment of the outcome of this ISO 31000 project?

1202. How effective was the training you received in preparation for the use of the product/service?

1203. How effective was the acceptance management process?

1204. What is the distribution of authority?

1205. How useful and complete was the ISO 31000 project document repository?

1206. What were the major enablers to a quick response?

1207. What worked well or did not work well, either for this ISO 31000 project or for the ISO 31000 project team?

1208. How effectively and timely was your organizational change impact identified and planned for?

1209. How effective was the documentation that you received with the ISO 31000 project product/service?

1210. What is below the surface?

1211. Were all interests adequately involved/ informed?

1212. What is the growth stage of the organization?

1213. Is there any way in which you think your development process hampered this ISO 31000 project?

1214. How effective were Best Practices & Lessons Learned from prior ISO 31000 projects utilized in this ISO 31000 project?

1215. What is the value of the deliverable?

Index

Made in the USA
Columbia, SC
24 September 2021